100 Daily Acts of Friendship for Girls

A Devotional

100 DAILY ACTS OF

Friendship

for Girls

Julie Fisk | Kendra Roehl | Kristin Demery

Tyndale House Publishers
Carol Stream, Illinois

Visit Tyndale online at tyndale.com.

Visit Tyndale's website for kids at tyndale.com/kids.

Visit the authors' website at theruthexperience.com.

TYNDALE and Tyndale's quill logo are registered trademarks of Tyndale House Ministries. The Tyndale Kids logo is a trademark of Tyndale House Ministries.

100 Daily Acts of Friendship for Girls

Designed by Eva M. Winters

Edited by Deborah King

Published in association with the literary agency of Books & Such Literary Management, 52 Mission Circle, Suite 122, PMB 170, Santa Rosa, CA 95409.

For manufacturing information regarding this product, please call 1-800-323-9400.

For information about special discounts for bulk purchases, please contact Tyndale House Ministries at csresponse@tyndale.com, or call 1-800-323-9400.

ISBN 978-1-4964-4466-0

Printed in China

27   26   25   24   23   22   21
7   6   5   4   3   2   1

To our mothers and our daughters,
who inspired this book

Introduction

Friends can be what make us happiest . . . or craziest. They can encourage us, help us when we're going through hard things, and push us to be better. Or they can hurt us, lie to us about ourselves and others, disappoint us, and keep us from reaching out for new friendships.

If you're reading this, you're probably interested in good friendships. Maybe you've been bullied or had trouble making friends. Maybe you have good friends, but you still fight now and then or accidentally hurt each other's feelings.

But God made us to enjoy friendships. How do we do that in a culture that doesn't always support friendships or that sometimes encourages unhealthy ones? We start by recognizing that friendship was created by God to honor him and benefit us. No matter what happens in life or how friends may fail us at times, he never will. He will always remain our faithful friend and the one we can learn from and talk to about anything and everything.

Friendship "works" when we turn to what God says about healthy relationships and apply those truths to our friendships. What does God say about how anger, conflict, disappointment, jealousy, and competition harm our friendships and what we can do in those situations? We can find ways to be a good friend when life is hard or confusing or uncertain. Living God's way, we celebrate when our friends succeed, when they win, and when life is amazing.

This devotional will help you think through and find answers for the hard questions about friendship, help you build stronger friendships, and give you ideas for ways to celebrate your friends. Check out the Friendship in Action sections for fun activities you can do to strengthen your friendships or start new ones!

Honesty in Friendship

JULIE

> Wounds from a sincere friend are better than
> many kisses from an enemy.
>
> PROVERBS 27:6

"I am so angry. What was McKinsey thinking? I'm never talking to her again!" Adrienna slammed her locker a little harder than usual as she turned to Brittany.

"I don't think McKinsey knew that Ciara has been spreading rumors about you when she invited her along to the movie. I think she was trying to help you guys work things out, not betray you," Brittany said. "You can't be mad at someone who didn't know the whole story and was trying to be kind."

Adrienna frowned. It hurt a little that Brittany didn't agree with her, that Brittany was sticking up for McKinsey instead of her. "I don't know. Maybe McKinsey's just as bad as Ciara," she said.

"McKinsey's been a good friend," Brittany reminded Adrienna. "You don't want to ruin that by jumping to conclusions. Remember that other time, with Lisa?"

That had been a bad mistake—a time Adrienna's hasty temper had gotten her in trouble and nearly lost her a friend. Adrienna sighed. "I guess you're right. Thanks, Brittany."

Brittany smiled, and they walked together toward the doors leading to the bus line.

When we have a friend who loves us enough to correct us, we should not take that blessing lightly. It is so much easier not to confront than it is to gently hold our friends accountable. But the Bible teaches us that true friends will call us out on our wrong actions, unlike false friends who may speak sweet words even as they push us to make choices Jesus doesn't want us to make.

Wouldn't you rather hear truth spoken in love from friends and family than listen to the fake sweetness of those who don't really care about you? But that requires wisdom on our end. We have to be willing to listen with an open heart, to accept correction, and to recognize that our friends and family are on our side, even when they tell us that we were wrong. Hearing truth may feel painful in the moment, but it's the only way that we can grow.

Things to Think About

Have you been ignoring a painful truth someone you love has shared with you sincerely and with your best at heart?

Have you been avoiding a painful conversation with someone you love about their behavior?

❄ DAILY ACT OF FRIENDSHIP ❄

Make a promise to your friends to tell one another the truth when they are doing or saying something ungodly or unwise.

The New Girl

Love your neighbor as yourself.
MATTHEW 19:19

"Dear God, please send me a friend," Jamie prayed, looking around the crowded middle school cafeteria. Her stomach knotted as she looked from table to table, full of students laughing and talking. Everyone seemed to already have their own friend groups—and none of them noticed Jamie standing by herself.

Jamie's family had just moved to this town. She hadn't wanted to leave her old hometown and everything that was familiar. Even after a few weeks at the new school, she still hadn't met anyone to talk to. Jamie started heading toward a lunch table in the corner. Maybe no one would notice if she sat there by herself.

"Hey, Jamie!"

Jamie turned to see Alisha, a girl from her local church.

"Want to sit with me?" Alisha asked. She nodded toward a nearby table.

Jamie followed Alisha to the table.

Over the next few weeks, Jamie started seeing Alisha more and more. They sat together in English class, and Jamie found Alisha in math. Soon Alisha introduced Jamie to other girls as well. Alisha was God's answer to Jamie's prayer.

Being the new girl is hard, but it can also make us pay attention in other situations where someone else might be new as well as feeling a little lonely. Even if you've never been the new girl, you can imagine what it would be like to walk into an unfamiliar place where you didn't know anyone. When we put ourselves in someone else's shoes, we are practicing compassion for others. When we take that compassion and act on it by including someone who is new or feeling left out, we put our faith into practice.

The Bible says we are to love our neighbor the same way we love ourselves. What if when you started a sports team or new school activity, you kept an eye out for someone else who is new? A simple smile and hello can help someone else feel welcome when they feel out of place. Who knows what could happen when we take that small step? We might make a really good friend.

Things to Think About

Have you ever been the new girl at school, at church, or in the neighborhood? How were you welcomed by others?

Can you think of someone who is new to your school, your church, or a program you are a part of?

❀ DAILY ACT OF FRIENDSHIP ❀

Look for someone who is new, whether at school, at church, or in the neighborhood, and be willing to say hello and include them in your group.

Friendship in Action

Plan a game night at your house and invite someone who is new to your school or town.

The Heart of a Friendship

> The LORD doesn't see things the way you see them.
> People judge by outward appearance,
> but the LORD looks at the heart.
>
> 1 SAMUEL 16:7

"Cannonball!" Chloe's voice echoed off the backyard trees as she bounced up and off the diving board, tucking her feet underneath to make the biggest splash possible.

Surfacing, she heard the pool gate squeak as her best friend Dakota closed it behind her.

"Did you get a new swimsuit?" Chloe asked. "It's so cute!"

Chloe liked her own swimsuit just fine. But watching Dakota walk toward the pool, she couldn't help but think that Dakota's new gray tankini looked prettier and much more flattering than Chloe's faded yellow-and-purple floral swimsuit.

As Dakota jumped in the water and made her way toward Chloe, a bit of jealousy curled through Chloe, clouding the day. Instead of enjoying the sunny skies, sparkling blue water, and bright blue tiles under her feet, all Chloe could see was her own outdated swimsuit. Compared to Dakota, Chloe felt plain and awkward, and it spoiled her good mood.

But as the day wore on, Chloe gradually forgot about the jealousy she felt, instead focusing on the refreshing pool and how much fun she always had with Dakota.

We need to be happy for our friends when they have nice things, while also remembering that nice things are not what make us important or worthwhile. Like Chloe, you may sometimes wish things were different, and the world around us doesn't make it any easier. Advertisements show us trendy clothes, beautiful people, and cool toys and gadgets. But instead of wishing we could possess something our friend owns or look the way she does, we need to remember that nothing can ever have greater importance than the inward beauty God gave us.

God made us the way we are—on purpose!—and he doesn't make mistakes. In fact, he doesn't see things the way we do at all—because he is looking at our heart. When he looks at us, he sees beauty, whether we're wearing the latest fashions or a piece we've owned for a while. Let's intentionally focus on the beauty of our friendships instead of worrying about what we have or how we look.

Things to Think About

Do you ever get jealous of your friends? How do you respond when you're tempted to compare yourself with someone else?

What are some things about you that your friends value? What does God say about you?

❈ DAILY ACT OF FRIENDSHIP ❈
The next time you feel jealous,
remind yourself of the reasons you like your friend for
who she is, regardless of what she owns or looks like.

Speak Up

> [The devil] has always hated the truth,
> because there is no truth in him.
>
> JOHN 8:44

"Mom, can we talk?" Ling's heart pounded as her mom paused and looked up from washing the dishes.

"What's up, sweetie?" Mom asked as she reached for the towel to wipe her hands.

"I think my friend Bella needs help," Ling whispered, starting to cry. "But she asked me to keep what she told me a secret."

"Oh, honey, let's talk." Ling's mom gave her a hug, and they sat down at the kitchen counter together. "Remember how we promised not to keep secrets if someone might get hurt?"

Ling nodded. "That's what I told Bella. And no one can help her if they never know."

The devil loves to lie to us and to our friends, making us feel alone, ashamed, and unloved. He may convince us that we need to keep scary thoughts and feelings secret or trick us into thinking we are the only one who feels that way. But there are some secrets that should not be secrets. When a friend asks us to keep a secret like that, we may feel trapped, because we want to be a good friend and keep our word, but we also want to tell an adult we love and trust so our friend can get help.

The best way to stop Satan's lies is to tell someone who knows God's truth. A parent, grandma or grandpa, aunt or uncle, pastor, teacher, or another adult you trust is the perfect person to help because they can remind us of the truth. If a friend tells you a secret that is dangerous or makes you uncomfortable, find an adult you love and ask for advice. It's important to share those kinds of secrets, because that's how we reject the devil's lies and choose truth instead.

Things to Think About

Who is an adult you can trust to talk to when you or your friend is struggling with a secret that feels dangerous or uncomfortable?

Are you keeping a secret that needs to be shared with an adult you trust and love? Go talk to them today.

❊ DAILY ACT OF FRIENDSHIP ❊

Make a plan with a trusted adult for what to do when you learn a secret that might be dangerous, and agree on what you will tell anyone who asks you to keep a secret.

Friendship in Action

Are you wondering if you should talk to an adult about a situation involving you or a friend?
The answer is yes if:

- someone tells you that another person is hurting them (either with their words or actions);
- someone is hurting you;
- you or a friend are having thoughts about hurting themselves; or
- any other time you are unsure. Check with a trusted adult.

A Second Home

KENDRA

Don't be concerned for your own good
but for the good of others.
1 CORINTHIANS 10:24

Mandy and Veronica met at church—and they hit it off quickly. It wasn't long before Veronica asked Mandy, "Would you want to come and hang out at my house?"

"Yes!" Mandy responded quickly. Mandy's dad did not live at home and her mom was gone and working a lot, so Mandy was lonely and in need of a friend. She was happy to be invited.

Veronica and her mom, Claudette, soon realized that Mandy's home life was hard. They began to invite Mandy to their home often. They'd bake together, do crafts, and just spend time together. Veronica and her mom would also pick up Mandy on Wednesday nights for church.

Over time Veronica's house became a second home for Mandy, a safe space where she was shown love, compassion, and kindness.

Sometimes we may meet someone whose family is not the safe shelter it should be. When we meet someone like that, God wants us to be there for them, to notice others who may be hurting and in need of a friend. We can be the one who is there for other people going through a hard time.

God doesn't want us to just be concerned for ourselves and our own lives, but to also be concerned for others. This means we can all be on the lookout for other kids and people around us who are sad and lonely. We can be the ones to take an interest in their lives and offer comfort and support to someone in need. We can make our circles of love a second home for them.

Things to Think About

Who has been there for you when you were going through a hard time? How did they show you they cared?

Who around you may be in need of a friend?

❋ DAILY ACT OF FRIENDSHIP ❋

Look for someone who is lonely and be the friend who'll listen and invite them into your circle of friends or family.

Choose Your Words

KRISTIN

> Those who control their tongue will have a long life;
> opening your mouth can ruin everything.
>
> PROVERBS 13:3

From Gabriella's bedroom window on the second floor, she could hear the neighbor girls gathered outside on the sidewalk. She and her friends had disagreed, and she'd stormed off.

Curious about what they were saying, Gabriella crept closer to the windowsill, careful not to let them see her peering out.

"Gabby's so bossy today," Lauren complained. "She thinks she's in charge."

Hearing the criticism made Gabriella's blood boil. Standing up abruptly, she faced the open window. "Shut up, Lauren, you brat!" Gabriella hollered. Her words echoed outside and through the house. Stunned silence greeted the angry shout.

Gabriella's sister Skylar ran into the room. "What's going on?"

As Gabriella turned to Skylar, she felt her rage shifting and bubbling over into tears. She felt sick inside over the way she had acted and the mean words she had yelled. Her temper had gotten the best of her, and now she had to face the consequences.

By the time Gabriella got her temper and tears under control, her friends had scattered. Ashamed, she headed to apologize to Lauren, now back at her own house.

Even when our friends accept our apology, we may still regret words said in a moment of anger. Words are powerful. Proverbs reminds us that if we aren't careful about what we say, the consequences can be long lasting. Words said in the heat of an argument can't be unsaid and can lead to lasting damage in our friendships. Though anger can make us feel ugly on the inside, we still have the power to say—or not say—hurtful words that match how we feel. Disagreements can often be resolved calmly if we choose our words wisely, and we won't have to apologize later on for the things we wished we hadn't said. Rather than using our words to wound a friend, let's use them to encourage and reassure one another. Those are words we'll never regret saying.

Things to Think About

How do you respond when you have a disagreement with a friend or overhear something negative about yourself? Do you choose your words wisely or struggle to not say something harsh in response?

Have you said something to a friend lately that you need to apologize for?

❋ DAILY ACT OF FRIENDSHIP ❋

The next time you feel angry with a friend, try a breathing exercise to calm you before you speak to your friend.

Friendship in Action

To ease anxiety, try this breathing exercise: Breathe in deeply through your nose while counting to four. Hold the breath for four counts. Release it through your mouth in four counts. Rest while counting to four, then start the exercise again. Imagine that you are tracing the sides of a square: 4, 4, 4, 4.

Frenemies

*There are "friends" who destroy each other, but
a real friend sticks closer than a brother.*
PROVERBS 18:24

"Marissa's kind of a frenemy," Liz said. She and her mom were walking their dog around the neighborhood, talking about Liz's day. Liz had shared with Marissa that she was worried about an upcoming test, and Marissa had made fun of her in front of their classmates.

"What do you think *frenemy* means?" Liz's mom asked gently.

Later, Liz and her mom looked up the word. The dictionary said it means "one who pretends to be a friend but is actually an enemy."

"Is that the kind of person you should be spending time with?" Liz's mom asked, putting an arm around Liz. "Is she really your friend?"

Liz thought for a minute. "I guess not," she said. "I want to be friends with Marissa, but Marissa seems more interested in being popular than in genuine friendship."

Most of us have accidentally hurt a friend's feelings and had to apologize. But are we truly a friend if we intentionally do something we know will hurt another person? Probably not, right? If you're wondering if someone is a frenemy, here are a few questions to ask:

1. How does she speak of others when they are not around? Does she make fun of others? Does she share someone's private information so she can feel popular?

2. How does she handle disagreements? Does she turn them into drama by trying to get others to take her side? Does she make a big deal out of little things so others will pay attention to her?
3. Does she tell lies or stretch the truth, even about small things?

We should be friendly to everyone because Jesus tells us to be kind and generous. However, we should also be careful in choosing with whom we share our deepest emotions. God tells us to be wise about who we have as friends. If you think a person is unsafe or a "frenemy," you can be kind to her, but still not give her access to your heart. And if you have ever acted like a frenemy yourself, today is a great day to begin acting like a true friend instead.

Things to Think About

When have you shared your heart with someone who is more frenemy than friend? What happened?

In what ways have you sometimes acted more like a frenemy than a friend?

❋ DAILY ACT OF FRIENDSHIP ❋

If you know a frenemy, be polite and kind but stop sharing your heart with her. If you've acted like a frenemy, write a note of apology.

Sharing One Another's Burdens

KENDRA

Don't look out only for your own interests,
but take an interest in others, too.
PHILIPPIANS 2:4

"What's wrong?" Ava asked as soon as she heard crying coming from one of the stalls in the bathroom. As Sophia emerged from the stall, Ava put a hand on her shoulder to comfort her. "Are you okay?" she asked.

"No," her classmate said shakily. "My dog just died this week."

Ava hugged Sophia and told her she could understand how sad she was, because her family dog had died as well. The girls shared about their pets as a way to comfort and support one another. After a few more minutes, the two clasped hands, left the restroom, and walked back to their class.

It can take just a few minutes to see another's hurt and show them compassion. We all have the ability to look around us at school, church, or other activities for someone who may be hurting and offer them a listening ear and tenderness. Scripture says we shouldn't only look out for our own interests, only be concerned with ourselves and our lives, but that we should care about others as well. Ava wasn't close friends with Sophia, but that didn't mean she would dismiss her pain. Ava understood what it was like to be in her shoes and, because of it, she could offer comfort.

Even if someone has experienced something we haven't, we can still imagine what that would be like and offer compassion. The world is full of people who turn away from others in their pain. As followers of Jesus, we can be the ones to show his love to people who are hurting.

Things to Think About

When others around you are hurting, do you notice?

How have you offered comfort to someone else?

Who has been a friend to you when you were going through a hard time?

❁ DAILY ACT OF FRIENDSHIP ❁

Offer comfort to a friend who is going through a hard time.

Friendship in Action

Make a handmade card for a friend who is going through a hard time and either send it in the mail or give it to them the next time you see them.

Tempted to Brag

If I must boast, I would rather boast about the things that show how weak I am.
2 CORINTHIANS 11:30

"You're here!" Audrey said, running to meet her friend Jocelyn at the curb. Jocelyn was visiting for the first time, and Audrey was eager to show her around.

"Your garage is *almost* as big as mine," Jocelyn said as they walked toward the house.

Audrey nodded, not sure what to say. She'd never thought about her garage very much. Maybe Jocelyn would like her room instead.

But as the tour continued, the comparisons did too. Jocelyn's house was bigger and newer. She had her own cell phone and had all kinds of popular, new toys that Audrey didn't have.

"Do you want to listen to music?" Audrey asked. "I can have my mom turn it on for us."

"Don't you have an Alexa in your room?" Jocelyn asked.

Audrey fell silent. It didn't matter what she said—Jocelyn always had something better. She was stumped.

Sometimes when people are insecure, they will compare themselves to others to make themselves seem stronger. But comparisons can be hurtful, and when we talk about what we own in a way that makes others feel left out, it can ultimately harm our friendships. After all, it's not the things we have that define us, but how we treat others.

It takes a lot more bravery for us to talk about what we lack than to talk about the parts of our lives that make us strong or happy. The Bible reminds us that if we're going to brag about anything, it should be our weaknesses, because it's through them that people are able to see the power of God at work. When we look back at problems we have overcome, seeing the way God helped us can strengthen our faith. And, it's only when we admit our weaknesses that we allow others to see the real us. If we're willing to share the hard parts of our lives with our friends instead of bragging about the easy parts, it will strengthen our faith and our friendships.

Things to Think About

Think of a time when a friend bragged. How did you respond?

What does it mean to "boast" about our weaknesses? What might that look like?

❋ DAILY ACT OF FRIENDSHIP ❋

List three of your strengths and three areas you are challenged in. Talk to a friend you trust about a weakness or struggle in your life.

Powerful Prayers

> The LORD is close to all who call on him, yes,
> to all who call on him in truth.
> PSALM 145:18

"Oh, Jesus, please help me," McKenna prayed. "I think Tara is angry at me, but I don't know why, and I don't know what to do about it. Please help me. Please help Tara. I don't want to lose her as a friend."

Tara and McKenna have been friends for a long time. When Tara started avoiding McKenna, McKenna knew something was bothering her, but Tara clearly didn't want to talk about it, so McKenna didn't know what it was or how to fix it. She was sad and a little angry that Tara wouldn't talk to her, so she did the only thing she could; she prayed.

A week later, Tara wrote McKenna a note: *Some really hard things have been happening in my life. I don't want to talk about it right now, but please pray for me.*

McKenna wrote her a note back: *You mean so much to me as a friend. I pray that God would watch over you and help you every day.* McKenna hoped Tara would carry that prayer with her and reread it whenever she needed encouragement.

When McKenna saw Tara the next day, they gave each other a giant hug. Tara knew McKenna was there for her and would be there when she was ready to talk.

It isn't always easy being a friend. Friendship is about far more than the fun sleepovers and hangouts. It's also about recognizing when our friend is struggling and supporting her even when our own feelings are sad and confused. Oftentimes, the hard things our friends struggle with are things we cannot fix, and we can feel useless and small.

Did you know our prayers are powerful? The Bible tells us over and over that God hears our prayers, he is close by when we pray, and he responds to our prayers. Jesus reminds us to pray for our friends, for ourselves, and for the world around us. Too often it's the thing we try last, but prayer is really the most powerful tool we have when our friends are going through a tough time.

Things to Think About

Think of a time you were struggling. What would have helped you? How would you have wanted your friends to react? What would you have wanted your friends to pray for?

Which of your friends currently needs your prayers?

❄ DAILY ACT OF FRIENDSHIP ❄

Make a pretty card with a handwritten prayer for a friend and slip it into her locker or binder. Make it a weekly habit to give a friend a written prayer.

Friendship in Action

Gather your craft supplies and create a beautiful card for a friend. Write her a note and include a short prayer in the card.

Who's Influencing You?

Don't be fooled by those who say such things,
for "bad company corrupts good character."
1 CORINTHIANS 15:33

"Mom, you need to come and get me," Susan said into the phone. Her heart sank. She knew she'd been caught and felt horrible. As she sat in the mall security office waiting for her mom to arrive, she wondered how she ended up here.

Several months earlier, Susan had started spending time with a girl who liked to shoplift. At first, Susan was alarmed at her friend's behavior, but over time she saw all the things her friend was getting and how she never got caught. It started to look appealing. One day when they were out together, Susan took a small pair of earrings and slipped them in her bag—nothing too expensive. As she left the store, she felt excited that she'd gotten away with a new pair of earrings—ones she didn't have to pay for.

As time went on, it got easier to steal more often and more things— until Susan got caught. She had several shirts and a sweatshirt in her bag, more than she'd ever tried taking before. Her mom came to the security office, shocked and disappointed by what her daughter had done, and took her home. Over the next several months, Susan paid back the store for all that she'd taken and vowed to never steal again. And she never did.

You may not have stolen something from a store, but all of us are vulnerable to doing things we wouldn't otherwise if we spend too much time with—and allow ourselves to be influenced by—people who make poor choices.

When we look around at our friends, the question we need to ask ourselves is *Who is influencing whom?* Are we a positive influence for those around us, encouraging others in beneficial ways? Or do we allow ourselves to go along with the crowd, even when we know it's wrong? No one is perfect, including us or our friends. Sometimes we'll make mistakes or do the wrong thing. But one of the best decisions we can make is to be wise about who we allow to get close enough to influence our thoughts, words, and actions.

Things to Think About

Who are your closest friends? How are they influencing you?

Are they encouraging you in positive or negative ways?

❋ DAILY ACT OF FRIENDSHIP ❋

Look for a way to be a positive influence
on the friends around you.

Why We're Kind Anyway

KRISTIN

> Love your enemies! Do good to them. Lend to them
> without expecting to be repaid. Then your reward
> from heaven will be very great, and you will truly
> be acting as children of the Most High, for he is kind
> to those who are unthankful and wicked.
>
> LUKE 6:35

"Marie, it's time for bed," her mom said, pausing at the door.

Seated at the small table, Marie didn't even look up. She remained intent on the project in front of her, working steadily. "I know, Mom. I'm almost done."

It was the night before the last day of school, and Marie was making twenty personalized cards for her classmates. Finally satisfied with how they turned out, Marie licked the last envelope closed and carefully slid the cards into a plastic bag in her backpack. She couldn't wait to give them out.

But things didn't turn out the way Marie had expected. As she shrugged out of her backpack after school the next day, her mom called her over to ask how the school day went.

"Pretty well," Marie said, biting her lip.

Her mom waited, listening.

"Some of the kids ripped my cards into shreds, and some made them into paper airplanes that they threw across the room," Marie admitted.

"I'm sorry," her mom said, drawing her into a hug. "What did your friends do?"

"Well, they kept them." Marie smiled. "I guess that's what matters."

It hurts when we try to do a kind act for someone and they reject it. The truth is, we can control our own actions, but we can't control someone else's response. Not everyone is going to accept our attempt to be their friend, but we can still choose to be friendly to everyone.

Jesus demonstrated kindness to all people, whether they were kind to him or not. When we choose to be kind, we reflect the love of Jesus to the world. Yet even as we choose kindness, we recognize that not everyone will be a friend in return. The times when it is reciprocated simply makes us all the more grateful for the friends who do show us love and acceptance.

Things to Think About

Have you ever had someone respond in an unkind way when you were trying to be a friend? How did you react?

Knowing what you know about Jesus and his example, how might you respond next time?

❄ DAILY ACT OF FRIENDSHIP ❄
Create something to give to a friend.
You could make her a bracelet or scrunchie or
bake something like banana bread or brownies.

Friendship in Action

Choose one kind thing to do for a friend today. Consider the list below:

- Loan them your favorite book, movie, or toy.
- Bring an extra treat to share at lunch.
- Draw a picture of the two of you together.
- Compliment them on something you like or appreciate about their personality or friendship.

A Boy-Friend Named Jonny

JULIE

Two people are better off than one,
for they can help each other succeed.
ECCLESIASTES 4:9-10

"Jonny and Krista sitting in a tree, K.I.S.S.I.N.G." Lucas sing-songed to Jonny as he walked past the lunch table.

"Ignore him, Jonny," Krista said as she took a bite of her pizza.

Jonny slumped over his tray. "It's hard to ignore him—he's been singing that annoying song all week. And now other kids are starting to sing it too."

"Do you want to stop sitting together at lunch? Maybe we can be secret friends but ignore each other at school."

For a minute, Krista thought maybe he'd agree. But then Jonny shook his head. "No way, Krista. Boys and girls can be friends without everyone shipping them. If he keeps doing that, I'll tell Ms. Jones."

Krista sighed in relief. Jonny was a smart and kind friend to her, someone with a different perspective on life simply because he is a boy. And she thought her perspective was helpful to him when he asked her for advice in return. "Good plan. Now tell me more about this Star Wars movie marathon you are planning for next weekend. I want to come."

Jonny is a friend who is a boy—not a boyfriend. So often, the message we hear in movies, books, and on social media is that it isn't possible to simply be friends with boys. And if we are, our classmates might tease us mercilessly by singing the "kissing in the tree" song or asking repeatedly if we are dating. Many people think that boys and girls cannot be friends unless romance is involved, but having that viewpoint might keep you from finding some great friends.

The right friends make our life better and help us succeed. And when we are friends with someone who is different than us in some way (like a boy), we can learn from that friend's ideas and experiences and make better decisions. So don't let others' teasing stop you from being a good friend to someone—just because that friend is a boy.

Things to Think About

When have you teased others who have a friend who is a boy, or allowed classmates to do the same? How do you think that made them feel?

How have your friendships with boy classmates, neighbors, or church kids made your life happier?

❀ DAILY ACT OF FRIENDSHIP ❀

The next time you see someone being teased, step in and direct the attention to something else.

Being Friends with Yourself

KENDRA

> See how very much our Father loves us,
> for he calls us his children, and that is what we are!
> 1 JOHN 3:1

"I'm so clumsy!" Colette said as she wiped ice cream that had dripped down the front of her shirt.

Grandma Dana put an arm around Colette's shoulders. "As a girl, I could be very mean to myself," she told Colette. "I would often criticize why I had said a certain thing or why I didn't look a certain way."

Colette took a lick of her ice cream. "I guess I do that too," she whispered.

Her grandma nodded. "As I've gotten older, I realized it wasn't helping me feel good about myself and it didn't help me achieve what I wanted to do. If anything, it held me back in fear."

"So what did you do?" Colette asked.

"I started really reading the Bible," Grandma Dana said with a smile. "I realized what I was telling myself wasn't what God would say to me. They weren't truths from his Word—they were lies. They were also things I would never say to a good friend. I would never want to hurt someone else with the kinds of things I was telling myself."

Colette nodded. "Can you show me the Scriptures you read?"

"Of course!" her grandma replied. "I'll make you a list when we get home."

God does not hide his feelings about us. The Bible says that we are loved, chosen, forgiven, and created with purpose. When we begin to ask him to help us, listen to his voice (instead of our own), and hear what he has to say about us, our thoughts about ourselves can change.

We'll become more secure in who we are, because we can be secure in what God thinks about us. We are God's beloved children! Once we know how much God loves and is for us, we can choose to believe his truth and be a good friend by speaking kind words over ourselves—and over our friends.

Things to Think About

Have you ever put yourself down? What kinds of things have you said?

Do you know what God thinks about you?

Make a list of the true things God says about you.

❋ DAILY ACT OF FRIENDSHIP ❋

When you start to put yourself down,
replace that thought with a truth from God's Word.

Friendship in Action

Look up these five truths about who God says you are as a person:

- You are loved. (John 3:16; Jeremiah 31:3; 1 John 3:1)
- You are worthy. (Zephaniah 3:17)
- You are valuable. (Luke 12:6-7)
- You have a purpose. (Jeremiah 29:11; Romans 8:28; Ephesians 2:10)
- You are unique. (Psalm 139:14)

Pick the verse you needed to hear most today and write it on your mirror using a dry-erase marker (with an adult's permission) as a reminder.

Trouble at the Amusement Park

KRISTIN

Share each other's burdens, and
in this way obey the law of Christ.
GALATIANS 6:2

"Come on, let's go on Ghost Blasters next!"

Elise hurried to keep up with her friends. She had already braved the scariest roller coaster—The Rock Bottom Plunge—and ridden countless times on Brain Surge, where she flipped upside down, round and round, and backwards. So when her friends asked if she wanted to ride Ghost Blasters, she was confident it would be fun.

Elise tapped her toes as they waited. The closer she got to the front of the line, the scarier the ride looked. It was dark inside and had creepy ghosts with gaping white faces on it. Elise tried not to feel worried, but as she buckled into the ride, she felt even worse. Her two friends were riding together, which meant she was alone. As the ride began, Elise wished that she had never agreed to go. Scary images flashed by, and she covered her eyes and started to cry.

"Elise, what's wrong?" her friend asked as they exited the ride, noticing her wet and puffy eyes.

"I got scared," she admitted. She paused, then gathered her courage. "Are you guys afraid of anything?"

"I'm scared of heights," one said, wiggling her eyebrows up toward the roller coasters.

"I'm scared of snakes," the other said, shuddering a little.

As the three friends headed back toward Brain Surge, Elise felt better, knowing that her friends were afraid sometimes too.

It takes courage to be the one to admit when we're the one who is scared, sad, or worried about something in our life. It can be easier to ignore our feelings, especially when we don't know how someone else will respond. Yet when we tell a friend how we truly feel—as Elise did— we'll often find that they will admit to their own struggles. As friends, we're asked to share each other's burdens, helping one another feel better about the things that weigh us down. Sharing the feelings or situations that trouble us reminds us that what we face and feel are normal, and that—with friends by our side—we are never alone.

Things to Think About

What are some of the things that worry you or make you afraid?

Have you shared them with a friend? What was their response?

❀ DAILY ACT OF FRIENDSHIP ❀

Make a list of three items or situations that scare you.
Find out what scares your friends and
notice what you have in common.

Don't Believe Lies

JULIE

> Their mouths are full of cursing, lies, and threats.
> Trouble and evil are on the tips of their tongues.
>
> PSALM 10:7

"Honey, I'm confused. You enjoy math even though it's a little harder for you. Why is math the lowest grade on your report card?" Layla's dad asked as they drove to soccer practice.

Bursting into tears, Layla confessed that she hadn't been doing her computer math homework. She'd quit after classmates noticed her slower than average progress and started telling her she shouldn't bother because she was terrible at math.

Her dad reached a hand into the back seat for a quick pat on her knee, "Do NOT let them steal your future. They are telling you lies."

As Layla wiped her tears, her dad asked if she had heard the story of the crabs in the bucket. "The story goes like this. If there is only one crab in a small bucket, it can easily climb out and escape. But when there is more than one crab in a bucket, they focus on pulling down any crab attempting to climb out and all wind up on the dinner plate!"

Some people are like the crabs in the bucket. They pick at people's weaknesses, tearing down everyone around them because of their own insecurity and hurt. If they can make others feel bad, they feel good—even for just a little bit. But when we let people like that influence what we do, we give them a lot of power over our future!

The devil will sneakily use the hurtful words of others to stop God's plans for us. He wants us to believe lies and give up trying to do our best. But we have the choice to be kind, compassionate people who, at the same time, do not allow the words of others to steal our future choices.

Being girls who love and follow Jesus requires us to recognize and ignore the lies offered by a hurting, insecure world.

Things to Think About

When have you quit trying after someone teased you? List three emotions you felt.

When have you teased someone about not being very good at something that comes easily to you? How did you feel afterward?

❋ DAILY ACT OF FRIENDSHIP ❋

Ask God to help you know the difference between wise advice from those who love you and the poisonous lies sent by the enemy to try to keep you from God's plans for your future.

Friendship in Action

Gather your friends and use watercolors to paint a beautiful background on a piece of paper or canvas. Once that is dry, use a permanent marker to write sentences you know God says are true about you. Hang your painting somewhere you can see it every day. Start with these truths:

- I am a child of God. (John 1:12)
- I am a friend of Jesus. (John 15:15)
- I am forgiven. (Ephesians 1:7)
- God takes care of me. (Philippians 4:19)

Now it's your turn. What else does Scripture say about you? Make it a contest to see how many Bible truths you and your friends can add to your artwork.

What Is She Not Saying?

> Work at living in peace with everyone,
> and work at living a holy life, for those
> who are not holy will not see the Lord.
> HEBREWS 12:14

"Where's Maya?" LaTasha's mom asked as she walked through the door.

"She said she doesn't want to walk me home anymore," LaTasha said.

"How come?"

LaTasha looked at the floor instead of her mom's eyes. "I guess I teased her about liking a boy in our class." Then she quickly added, "But it wasn't a big deal, Mom. I don't know why she was so upset about it."

"It must have been a big deal to her if she said she doesn't want to walk home with you anymore. Even if you don't think it's a big deal, if it seems like it's upsetting your friend, it's time to stop. We need to be sensitive to the feelings someone is showing and not just their words."

As her mom spoke, LaTasha began to see how her friend Maya had been showing signs of being upset long before she had said anything. Immediately LaTasha felt ashamed for not noticing it earlier.

"It's okay," her mom said. "That's all part of learning and growing up. Now that you know, just go back to her, apologize, and make it right."

And that's just what LaTasha did the very next day.

We can all miss the nonverbal things friends are saying, but it's important for us to watch how others react to our words and stay sensitive to how they may be feeling, even when they don't say it out loud. We need to ask ourselves: *Do they appear upset? Are they laughing with me or have they become quiet?* Someone's behavior is often just as important as the words they share. If we want to be a good friend to others, we need to read their body language as well as listen to their words.

As girls who love Jesus, we are meant to live at peace with others. Noticing their reactions to our words and asking forgiveness for offenses when necessary is all part of living a godly life.

Things to Think About

Have you thought about the ways people react without saying a word?

What kinds of things do people say with their nonverbal cues? How would you know if you were hurting someone's feelings even if they didn't tell you?

❈ DAILY ACT OF FRIENDSHIP ❈

Notice the way your friends respond to
your words with their nonverbal reactions.
Adjust what you say to show you care.

Wishing for Popularity

KRISTIN

> Give all your worries and cares to God,
> for he cares about you.
>
> 1 PETER 5:7

Sorting through the papers Annie had brought home from school, her stepmom noticed one titled "My Wishes." Underneath, Annie had drawn pictures of herself and the things she wished were true.

Annie's second wish read: "Be popular."

"Why do you want to be popular?" her stepmom asked.

Annie hesitated. "Because I feel lonely at school," she admitted.

Annie's best friend had moved to another school district the year before. No one at school was mean—they just had friends already, so she was often left out.

Her stepmom nodded. "Sometimes I feel lonely too—when I focus on the people I'm not friends with. But then I remember the people I do have in my life. Can you think of anyone?"

"I had fun in gym class with Lara last week," Annie admitted. "And Grace gave me a bracelet she made yesterday." As she thought about it, she realized she did have friends—but focusing on being popular had made her forget.

Everyone feels lonely sometimes. It's important to notice when other people are on the fringes and invite them in. But what happens when we're the one on the fringe? Annie's desire to be popular isn't uncommon. Don't we all want to be liked? Admired? Not alone?

It's important to recognize the friendships that are already there—waiting for us. And if we're lonely, it's also important to remember that we can pray specifically for God to send us friends. God cares about the big and the small details of our life, and friendships are no exception. We can give our worries and fears to him, knowing that he cares for us.

Things to Think About

What does "popular" mean to you? Have you ever felt lonely or wished for friends?

How does bringing our fears and worries to God change our response to loneliness and friendships?

❋ DAILY ACT OF FRIENDSHIP ❋

Bring an extra treat with you to school. At lunchtime, ask someone you don't normally sit with to sit next to you. Share the extra treat with them.

Friendship in Action

Here's an easy recipe for a sweet, crispy-crusted apple bread you can bake at home and share with a friend. Don't forget to ask an adult before using the oven or invite the adult to help you.

ANNIE'S APPLE BREAD

Ingredients:

- 2 eggs
- ½ cup vegetable oil
- 2 teaspoons vanilla
- 2 cups flour
- 2 cups sugar
- 1 ½ teaspoons salt
- 1 teaspoon baking powder
- ½ teaspoon cinnamon (or more, if desired)
- 2 cups apples (peeled and diced)

Directions:

- Preheat the oven to 350 degrees. Grease an 8.5" by 5.5" bread pan well (or use four small ones).
- Mix the wet ingredients (eggs, oil, and vanilla) together in a large bowl.
- In a separate bowl, mix the dry ingredients (flour, sugar, salt, baking powder, and cinnamon) together.
- Combine the wet and dry ingredients, then add the diced apples and mix well.
- Bake the bread for 45–60 minutes. Test it with a toothpick for doneness. (If it comes out clean, it's done.)
- Cool the bread in the pans for 10 minutes, then run a knife around the edges before removing and transferring the loaves to a wire rack to finish cooling.

A Dance Duet

JULIE

How good and pleasant it is when God's
people live together in unity!

PSALM 133:1, NIV

"Laura, do you want to sign up for a duet with me?" Kinsey asked one of her best friends as they added their names to the audition list for the advanced dance team.

"Oh, that sounds cool! Yes, go for the duet. I am so excited for this dance season!" Laura replied.

Kinsey and Laura met when they joined the same dance studio several years earlier and became close friends. When Kinsey saw the chance to dance a duet together, she was so excited!

But a week later her heart sank when she realized she had made the advanced team and Laura had not. It hadn't occurred to either of them that they would ever be on separate dance teams. Kinsey wasn't sure what to say to Laura. She was proud of herself for making the most competitive team, but she was worried that Laura would feel abandoned or sad and not want to participate in their duet.

Kinsey turned to her mom for advice and texted Laura, telling her how badly she still wanted to dance the duet together despite being on different teams. Kinsey worked to find the right balance of encouraging Laura without giving up her own dream of being on the more competitive team. Laura had to find the right balance of excitement for Kinsey while remaining confident in her own abilities and willing to dance the duet. Both girls had to choose friendship over uncomfortable feelings and learned to support one another instead of letting competition and insecurity get in the way.

One of the hardest parts of friendship to navigate is when our talents separate us from our friends. We might find ourselves in the advanced English class, making the basketball team, or being selected for a lead role in the play, or perhaps our friend is selected and we are not.

It's okay to be quietly disappointed but still filled with joy for someone else. We can't let disappointment ruin our friendships. God gives talents and giftings to each of us, and we discover or develop those talents at different times. God doesn't want our friendship and unity destroyed as we discover our different gifts.

Things to Think About

What talent or gift does your friend have that you've wished for?

Make a list of the talents and gifts you have that others don't have.

❀ DAILY ACT OF FRIENDSHIP ❀

Write a note to your friend listing
three things she does well.

DAY 20
Generous Friendship
KENDRA

Some people are always greedy for more,
but the godly love to give!
PROVERBS 21:26

"Honey!" Luna's mom poked her head in the door of Luna's bedroom. "I just talked to Mrs. Jones on the phone. She said you'd given Annamarie your Darcy doll."

"She didn't have a doll, Mom, so I thought I'd give her one of mine. I still have more," Luna explained.

Her mom sat beside Luna and put an arm around her shoulder. "I'm a little surprised, since you loved that doll. But I understand your desire to be generous with a friend who doesn't have one."

Luna hugged her mom back. "So many people have given me nice things, Mom. Jenna gave me that game I loved, and Aunt Dana sent me a new dance leotard. Mrs. Tate brought me over banana bread yesterday. I just wanted to share the love—like you and Dad have been teaching me."

Luna's parents have been teaching her about the importance of watching for the needs of others and looking for ways to meet them. She has experienced generosity in friendship and wanted to be sure to pass it along to others. It's a valuable trait in friendship, the ability to share what we have with those around us. The Bible says that some people just want more and more, but the godly are eager to give! We've probably all known others who were stingy or greedy, but that is not what God asks of us as Christians.

There is more than one way to share with others. We can be generous with our time, our encouragement, our prayers, our listening, or even the things we have, like Luna's doll. No matter how we share, when we are giving, we show others the love of God in us. It's a skill we can develop no matter how young or old we are.

Things to Think About

Who has been generous in friendship to you? How were they giving toward you?

Who have you been generous toward? In what ways have you shared with them?

❇ DAILY ACT OF FRIENDSHIP ❇

Find a way to be generous (with your time, words, or possessions) in friendship toward someone else.

Friendship in Action

A DIY (DO IT YOURSELF) LIP BALM

Make a batch of this lip balm with a trusted adult. It makes enough to share with a friend!

Ingredients:

- 1 tablespoon shea butter (Cocoa butter or mango butter will also work.)
- 2 tablespoons coconut oil
- 1 tablespoon sweet almond oil
- 1½ tablespoons beeswax (Pellets are the easiest.)
- Essential oils of choice (lemon, peppermint, etc.)

Supplies:

- Small saucepan with double boiler or a microwave-safe bowl
- Wire whisk
- Pipettes
- Lip balm tubes (Lip balm tubes are available online, but you can also use small glass jars or reuse lip balm containers you have on hand.)

Directions:

- Melt and combine the shea butter, coconut oil, sweet almond oil, and beeswax on the stove or in the microwave.
  - On the stove: Add about an inch of water to a small pan. Place on stove over medium heat. Melt the ingredients in the double boiler. Whisk to combine.
  - In the microwave: Heat the ingredients in a microwave-safe bowl in short, 15-second intervals, repeating until fully melted. Whisk to combine.
- Add 12 to 15 drops of essential oils of your choice to the mixture and whisk to combine. (Add more for a stronger scent.)
- Use a pipette to divide the liquid among your containers, filling them.
- While filling the containers, stir what's left in the bowl every so often, since it cools and hardens quickly.
- Let the balm set (with the caps off) for 12 hours. Label the containers if desired.

You're Good Enough

> Such love has no fear, because perfect love
> expels all fear. If we are afraid, it is for fear
> of punishment, and this shows that we have
> not fully experienced his perfect love.
>
> 1 JOHN 4:18

"Why do you always say that?" Miranda asked, nodding toward the message Gwen had just finished scrawling in her yearbook.

Confused, Gwen glanced back at the words she had hastily written before their first-hour class began. It was a typical end-of-the-year, I'll-miss-you message, but at the end she had tacked on the words: "Thanks for putting up with me!"

Mystified, Gwen looked back at Miranda, unsure what the problem was.

"I don't sit next to you because I have to," Miranda said quietly. "I sit here because I want to."

Gwen was stunned. She had meant the comment as a joke, but maybe there was some truth to her own words. After all, although the two girls had been sitting next to each other in choir for a few years and Gwen considered them friends, they weren't very close. *Did she really think Miranda—and her other friends, for that matter—were just "putting up with her"?*

It's easy to compare ourselves with others—even our friends—and wonder if we're "good enough." Other girls seem smarter, prettier, more popular, more confident, better at sports or school, or more natural-born leaders than we'll ever be. Instead of recognizing the qualities others admire in us, we focus on areas where we struggle. Often, the root of the worry we feel is fear. It's normal to be worried or afraid every once in a while, but we can combat our fears by seeing ourselves through God's eyes—and the way he sees us is wildly different from the way our culture does. The Bible says perfect love casts out fear. When we replace our fears with the recognition of God's perfect love for us, we can be confident in who we are and—in turn—we can be confident in who God made us to be.

Things to Think About

Have you ever felt like you needed to prove yourself to a friend or act a certain way so that someone would like you? What made you feel that way?

How can you respond in a positive way to fear or insecurity?

❋ DAILY ACT OF FRIENDSHIP ❋

Pray that God would show you how to see yourself the same way he sees you—as worthy of love and friendship. List three things that make you uniquely you.

Temporary Friends

I was a stranger, and you invited me into your home.
MATTHEW 25:35

"How exciting! We're on the way to Disney World too." Beth plopped down on a seat next to another girl at the airport. She loved making temporary friends—and the airport was a great place for it.

The girl smiled shyly, turning so Beth could better see her Disney-themed T-shirt.

"What rides do you want to go on?" Beth asked.

"Well, Space Mountain—" the girl began.

Just then, Beth's phone pinged. Glancing down at the text, she realized she hadn't told her mom that she had walked across the hallway in the airport terminal. "Whoops, just a second," Beth said as she sent her mom a quick text and waved when her mom looked in her direction. "Okay, what were you saying about Space Mountain? I've never been on that ride and have heard it's scary, is that true?"

We don't need to be an adult with a home of our own to extend a warm welcome to others. Showing hospitality can sound very formal and serious, don't you think? But it simply means being kind to someone you don't know very well without expecting anything in return. It could be sitting next to the new kid at the lunch table so she or he doesn't eat alone. It could mean inviting others to join a game of sand volleyball at the beach or a game of pickup soccer at the park. There are so many ways to show small kindnesses to others at school, at church, or at other activities, ways that don't cost anything and are not hard to do.

Why does Jesus ask us to practice hospitality? When we are kind and friendly to others we don't know well without expecting anything in return, we show our love for Jesus and show Jesus' love for others. Maybe you aren't comfortable *talking* about Jesus in your school or to strangers. But being kind without receiving anything in return is a powerful way to *show* Jesus to those around you without saying a word.

Things to Think About

Think of a time someone you didn't know was kind to you. What did he or she do? How did that make you feel?

Think of a time you showed kindness to someone you didn't know. What did you do? How did it change your day?

❀ DAILY ACT OF FRIENDSHIP ❀

Make a plan to invite someone you don't know well to sit at your lunch table or to join an activity with you.

Friendship in Action

Hold a Kindness Contest with your friends this week. Challenge each other to show kindness to a person they don't know well at least once a day for a week, and then throw a Kindness Party at the end of the week to share your stories and celebrate with snacks and a movie.

Work for Peace

KENDRA

God blesses those who work for peace,
for they will be called the children of God.
MATTHEW 5:9

Jade was on the phone with a friend who said unkind things about another girl in their class. She listened for a few minutes, then made a half-hearted, not-so-nice comment about the other girl too.

As she hung up the phone, her mom called her into the next room. "What's going on?" her mom asked as she sat down next to her.

Jade's shoulders fell as she explained. "Two girls in my class are fighting." The one she had spoken to on the phone had told the other girls in their class that they shouldn't be friends with the third girl.

Jade wasn't sure what to do. Feeling pressured, she'd joined in, saying something unkind, even though she knew it wasn't right. Tears sprang to her eyes as she felt the weight of regret for what she'd said.

Her mom gave her a hug and told her she could understand the confusion Jade felt. "The next time you get in a situation like that, try to be a peacemaker. Let the other girls know you want to be friends with both of them, and you won't listen to either girl talk badly about the other."

It isn't always easy to find a perfect solution, but as peacemakers, we can try to build a bridge of friendship among others. Scripture tells us God blesses us when we seek peace, and that we will be called children of God when we do so. When girls we know aren't getting along, we can be the ones to bring peace by not joining in or speaking badly about others and by befriending those who may be left out.

Things to Think About

Have you ever had friends or classmates who didn't get along? How
was the situation resolved?

How can you be a peacemaker when others are fighting or being
mean to one another? (Think about what kind of things make
someone a good peacemaker. Not gossiping or saying unkind
things about either person, not taking sides, being a good listener
and supporter of both people—all are examples of ways that we
can be peacemakers.)

❀ DAILY ACT OF FRIENDSHIP ❀

When you see two people who aren't getting along, take
one action step to be a peacemaker between them.

The Befriender

Be strong and courageous,
all you who put your hope in the LORD!
PSALM 31:24

"There's a new girl at school," Noelle announced while sitting at the kitchen island after school, crunching on sliced apples and peanut butter. "Her name's Ana. It's pronounced 'Ahh-na' but people keep saying it wrong. She corrects them, but she's kind of quiet and doesn't say much."

Noelle's mom looked over from where she was digging in the pantry. "Who does she sit with at lunch? Who does she play with at recess?"

Noelle looked down at the countertop, unsure. "I don't know," she mumbled.

"Maybe you can be her friend. She would probably like it if someone invited her to sit with them."

"Maybe," Noelle said, shrugging. She hadn't really thought too much about it.

A few days later, Noelle rushed through the door after school, making a beeline toward her dad. "I made a new friend!" she said. Her heart was thumping in a happy way.

"You did? What's her name?"

"Ana," she said. "She sat with us at lunch."

Noelle noticed her mom in the other room. She had heard the conversation. Noelle smiled as her mom winked at her.

As Christians who are friends with Jesus, we can share his love and friendship with others. The Psalms remind us that our hope is in God, and by understanding that truth, we can be strong and courageous. We're never alone. He is always with us, in every circumstance! And he gives us the strength and courage we need to be brave enough to reach out to others. When we take the time to notice others and are courageous enough to befriend them, our bravery and kindness may result in one of the best and most worthwhile gifts of all: a new friend.

Things to Think About

Can you think of a time when someone unexpectedly befriended you?

Why is it important to be a befriender?

❋ DAILY ACT OF FRIENDSHIP ❋

Be a befriender. Invite someone to your house after school or to a sporting event or concert.

Friendship in Action

Inexpensive ways to make a new classmate feel welcome:

- Introduce yourself.
- If they are alone in class, sit beside them to keep them company.
- Ask them questions to get to know them (where they are from, favorite activities, favorite music or movie).
- Ask if they'd like to play at recess or sit by you at lunch.
- Share a snack or treat with them (making sure to ask about food allergies first).

A Bully or a Blessing?

JULIE

> Out of the same mouth come praise and cursing.
> My brothers and sisters, this should not be.
> JAMES 3:10, NIV

"*Some* people might wear that brand, but I wouldn't be caught dead in it." Abby's comment was loud enough for Miriam to hear two desks over.

Miriam felt her body flush warm with embarrassment as she realized she was wearing a T-shirt from the brand Abby and her friends were loudly discussing. Everyone who could hear Abby's comment could see that Miriam was wearing a shirt with that logo on it.

"I don't think there's anything wrong with that brand," Katie said suddenly. "If someone likes it, why shouldn't they wear it?" Katie smiled at Miriam, and Miriam smiled back, grateful for Katie's friendship. Abby's opinion suddenly didn't feel so important after all.

Was Abby being mean? Yes. Abby might defend herself by saying that she wasn't talking to Miriam and might even argue that she wasn't even talking *about* Miriam because she didn't use her name. But everyone who heard the comment knew it was meant to be hurtful to Miriam.

When people use subtle insults like Abby did, this is a kind of bullying. And because this kind of bullying can be more easily hidden from adults, some girls become very, very good at insulting girls they are angry with or don't like in this way.

The book of James reminds us that the words we speak are powerful. We have the choice to encourage people or hurt them, and choosing to hurt others is a sin. Being mean in sneaky ways is just as wrong as insulting someone directly. Let's use our mouths to bless and stand up for others—instead of tearing them down.

Things to Think About

Think of a time someone bullied you with subtle insults. What did they say? How did you feel? What did others who overheard the conversation say?

What can you choose to say the next time you hear someone being a sneaky bully? How might you stand up for the person they are insulting? What adult could you tell?

❄ DAILY ACT OF FRIENDSHIP ❄

Listen for sneaky bullying at your school,
at your church, or with your friends. Speak up
when someone is being subtly insulted.

Filling the Friendship Gap

KENDRA

Listen to my prayer, O God. Pay attention to my plea.
PSALM 54:2

"What movie do you want to watch tonight?" Charlotte's dad said with a smile, holding up two of her favorites.

"*Tangled*," Charlotte responded, snuggling into the couch by her dad.

As the opening music swelled, Charlotte's dad gave her arm a squeeze. "Make any new friends at school today?"

Charlotte shrugged. Moving to a new town in middle school had been hard. She'd had good friends at her previous school, and they couldn't be replaced in a few days or weeks.

"Don't worry," her dad said. "It will come. Just give it time. I've been praying you'll find a few good friends."

"Me too," Charlotte said as she leaned against him and smiled. They'd had movie night and special snacks or just hung out for a while every night that week. She could tell he was trying hard to fill the gap for her while she was missing her old friends and hadn't made new ones yet.

Parents, grandparents, and other mentoring adults fill many roles, and one of them can be that of a friend. Charlotte's nightly movies with her dad didn't last too long before she eventually made some good friends at her new school. But his friendship was an answer to her prayer when she was lonely and really needed someone close.

You don't have to move to a new city to go through a time when you might be lonely and in need of a friend. When you feel that way, you can pray and ask God for a friend (this is a request he loves to answer!), knowing he loves to pay attention to our pleas. We can also seek out others (including trusted adults) to talk with about our desire for a good friend. Just like with Charlotte and her dad, we might find it is an adult friend or family member who fills a void when we are in need of a friend.

Things to Think About

Have you ever felt lonely and in need of a friend? Have you spent time in prayer asking God for a friend?

Who is an adult that you could confide in about your loneliness?

❋ DAILY ACT OF FRIENDSHIP ❋

If you are struggling with friendships, pray about it and then reach out to a trusted adult about your concerns.

Friendship in Action

Watch a favorite movie at home with someone in your family to build your friendship. Brainstorm your ideas: action, comedy, animated? If you have more than one movie you want to watch, have a movie marathon or spread out watching them all over a few special nights.

Refusing to Take Sides

KRISTIN

If it is possible, as far as it depends on you,
live at peace with everyone.
ROMANS 12:18, NIV

"Hey, I feel like I haven't seen Autumn lately," Gianna's mom said at the dinner table one night.

Looking down at her plate, Gianna glumly shrugged her shoulders. "We're not really getting along right now," she admitted.

As her mom gave her a sympathetic smile and rubbed her shoulder, Gianna tried to smile but couldn't manage it.

The truth was, she felt like she'd been abandoned. She and Autumn had a crush on the same boy, but because he was interested in Gianna, their other friends had taken Autumn's side against her. Even though Gianna hadn't done anything wrong, she suddenly found herself struggling in her friendships, as her core group of friends turned their backs and began to avoid her.

When they saw her at school or at the mall, they ignored her and pretended she no longer existed. Events weren't as fun to attend any longer, either, because Gianna had so few friends to spend time with while there. Gianna was miserable.

A few weeks later, Autumn apologized for letting her hurt feelings come between them, and Gianna forgave her. They became even better friends than they had been in the past. Though Gianna missed her other friends, she was glad she at least had Autumn to lean on.

It can be hard not to take up an offense for someone else. When someone we care about feels hurt, we often feel angry or upset on their behalf. As Christians, we are to be people of peace. It's important to note that we are asked to do so "if it is possible." Sometimes conflict is unavoidable, and there are times when people just aren't interested in making peace with us. There's an appropriate time to respectfully disagree with others, especially if we are asked to do or say something that doesn't honor God. When it comes to friendship, living at peace means being willing to admit when we're wrong, apologize, and forgive one another—that's what "as far as it depends on you" means. When two of our friends squabble, we need to be very careful not to jump to conclusions or choose sides. Instead, we should consider how we can help foster peace and healing among friends.

Things to Think About

Have you ever had a disagreement with some of your friends? In that situation, were you helping to bring peace to the situation or were you adding more drama?

How can you be a person of peace in the midst of friendship conflicts?

❁ DAILY ACT OF FRIENDSHIP ❁

The next time friends have a dispute, refuse to take sides.

Big Sister Tax

> A friend loves at all times, and
> a brother is born for a time of adversity.
> PROVERBS 17:17, NIV

"Marya, come down here right now. I need to talk to you."

Sighing, Marya recognized that she was in trouble by her grandma's tone of voice. "*It's probably because Josiah tattled on me,*" she thought. "Yes, Grandma. I'll be right down."

Marya has two younger brothers. While they mostly get along, sometimes they drive her crazy. When they are bugging her, she uses Big Sister Tax to bug them back. She waits until they are playing in their upstairs bedroom right before Grandma calls them to dinner and then blocks the top of the stairs with her body. She makes her brothers give her a hug on each step until they reach the bottom—twelve hugs. It's a great form of revenge because no younger brother wants to hug their sister twelve times in a row!

Grandma was waiting for her in the kitchen. "Your brothers will someday be bigger and stronger than you, Marya. You will someday need their help as adults. Why don't you work harder at being their friend instead of finding ways to frustrate and annoy them?"

Proverbs tells us that our brothers and sisters are intended to be there for us in times of trouble. Adult siblings can be some of our best friends because they grew up in the same house, understand us better than most other people, and often have really good advice when we're not sure what to do.

Did you know that one of the best predictors of whether brothers and sisters will be friends as adults is how well they played together as children? Siblings who enjoy hanging out with one another and who make an effort to find things in common to do are more likely to be good friends as adults. Life can be really hard, but having friends who grew up in the same family (brothers and sisters) is important when life is tough.

Things to Think About

How can you be a better friend to your siblings? If you don't have a sibling, is there a stepsibling, cousin, or another relative near your age who you can treat like a friend?

What common interests or hobbies can you share with your siblings or relative to start building a friendship?

❁ DAILY ACT OF FRIENDSHIP ❁

This week, start treating your siblings the same way you treat your best friend and see what happens.

Friendship in Action

Be a friend to your family members. Try one of these:

- Challenge someone in your family to a friendly contest like jumping rope, Hula-Hooping, H-O-R-S-E or another basketball game, or hopscotch.
- Spend time working on a puzzle or playing board or video games together.
- Offer to help cook a meal.
- Do a chore for a sibling or parent without being asked.

Celebrate Our Differences

KENDRA

God created human beings in his own image.
In the image of God he created them;
male and female he created them.
GENESIS 1:27

"Hi, my name's Jasmine," Jasmine said as she noticed a new girl who walked into their classroom at the beginning of the year. "I'm Elsie," the other girl responded shyly. Jasmine noticed right away that her new friend was a girl with Down syndrome.

Over the course of that year, Jasmine spent time playing with her new friend Elsie, inviting her to play tag, and talking with her about movies she was interested in. They went to a Star Wars movie together. Jasmine said that even though most of the time people were kind to Elsie, sometimes others appeared uncomfortable or didn't want her to be around them. This upset Jasmine. She knew how kindhearted Elsie was and wanted her to always know she was welcome, that she belonged. Jasmine continued her relationship with Elsie even after the school year ended.

It's not unusual to feel uncomfortable around others who are different from us, and it's okay to notice differences. Our differences are what make us unique. But we shouldn't stop at noticing *differences*. We can also get to know others to find out what we have in common. Jasmine realized pretty quickly how many common interests she and Elsie shared—the movies they both liked and the games they liked to play. Their similarities bonded their friendship.

No one should be left out for being different, because in some way or other we all are different. Instead, we should make everyone feel welcome.

The Bible says that all people are created in God's image, so everyone has value in his eyes. Since we are all made in God's image, we should celebrate all the ways we are unique. As girls who love Jesus, we can be the ones to welcome people in, even when others do not, because we see the value God has placed in each of us.

Things to Think About

How have you included someone who, on the surface, may have appeared different from you?

Maybe you often feel different from those around you. How have others included you?

❊ DAILY ACT OF FRIENDSHIP ❊

Include someone who is different from you but
in need of a friend, whether at school or in another activity.

Boy-Crazy Girls

*"I know the plans I have for you," says the LORD.
"They are plans for good and not for disaster,
to give you a future and a hope."*
JEREMIAH 29:11

Laurel was poking through some old cardboard boxes when she found a sealed shoebox she'd never seen before.

"Mom, what is this?" she called out, shaking it gently. Something rustled inside.

"Oh boy," her mom said, entering the room. "Those are my old notes from middle school." As her mom unsealed the box, Laurel crowded close. Notes spilled out, some creased into elaborate shapes, others hastily folded.

"Can I look at them?" Laurel asked.

"Sure."

As her mom left the room, Laurel grabbed the box and dumped it on her bed. As she read, she noticed the notes had a lot in common. They mentioned homework, tests, bands, choir, and sports. Some were snarky, poking fun. Others discussed plans for sleepovers or hanging out together after school.

But the majority of the notes focused—at least in part—on boys: whether or not Sara liked Ryan, or if Teresa was really over Matt.

Laurel piled the notes back into the box and went looking for her mom.

"I didn't realize you were so boy crazy," she teased, tossing the box on the kitchen counter.

Her mom rolled her eyes. "You have no idea. The funny thing is, none of those relationships ever lasted. But it sure did make for a lot of jealousy and heartbreak in my friendships. I wish my friends and I had focused more on ourselves—our plans for the future, or even for summer vacation—than on relationships that didn't last."

When we are with friends, what if we focused less on the relationship drama that pulls our attention and more on God's plans and our dreams? What if we spent less time consumed with boys and more time asking our friend what she wants to accomplish in the next year or something fun she'd like to try? Who we really are is defined by our relationship with Christ. He has a dream and a vision for our future. Let's encourage our friends—and ourselves—to be brave enough to pursue it.

Things to Think About

Have you ever found yourself pulled into girl drama, especially as it relates to boys? What could you do next time to shift the conversation to another topic?

What are some activities you enjoy? What is something you might like to do with your life?

❋ DAILY ACT OF FRIENDSHIP ❋

Write a friend a note. Talk about something specific and fun you'd like to try or your upcoming plans. Ask your friend to do the same.

Friendship in Action

In a journal or notebook, write some of your dreams and plans. Use the following Dreams and Plans Fill-in-the-Blank List to get started. (And consider asking a friend to share her answers too.)

- In ten years, I hope I _____.
- One place I'd like to visit is _____.
- Something I've never tried but would like to is _____.
- If I could have any job in the world, it would be _____.
- One friend I really admire is _____ because _____.
- My perfect day would include _____.
- One food I'd like to try is _____.
- My greatest dream (so far) is _____.
- If I could meet anyone in the world for dinner, it would be _____.

The First Sleepover

God loves a cheerful giver.
2 CORINTHIANS 9:7, NIV

"Um, Lizzie, I overheard our moms talking, and it sounds like my little sister is coming to our sleepover tonight." Jasmine swung her backpack off her shoulder and sat on the bus seat just behind Lizzie's.

"But we were planning to ride our bikes over to Sara's! That won't work if Elle is along," Lizzie said, turning back to look at Jasmine.

"I know." Jasmine frowned. "My mom has to go visit Great-Grandma in the hospital, and your mom offered to take Elle so she doesn't have to worry about a babysitter."

Lizzie frowned too. She'd been looking forward to hanging out with Sara. But then she remembered the first time she'd been to a sleepover. "Has Elle ever been on a sleepover before?"

"Not other than with her cousins," Jasmine replied.

"Well, let's make a list of fun things to do with Elle tonight, and we'll switch our plans with Sara to next Friday." Lizzie started digging for a pencil and paper excitedly. "Do you think she would like to build a blanket fort in the dining room?"

"Oh, yes! I loved blanket forts at her age. Do you still have a few dolls? She loves Polly Pockets."

Jasmine and Lizzie's plans worked. Elle had a wonderful first sleepover, and Lizzie's mom quietly pulled the girls aside the next morning to thank them for being so kind to Elle and making her first sleepover so special.

Younger siblings, cousins, neighbors, and kids at school love when older girls pay attention to them, listen to what they have to say, and include them in activities. They see you as the cool older girl (even if you don't think you are cool), and they will feel extra special when they get to be a part of whatever fun you're having. God asks us to be cheerful givers, girls who are generous toward others rather than secretly resentful and grumbling. This applies to your whole life and to everything you have and are—whether it's your time, your money, your talents, or your attention.

Things to Think About

Think of a time an older girl made it obvious she was reluctantly allowing you to tag along in what she was doing. How did that experience feel?

When did an older girl act generously toward you with her time and attention? How did her generosity make you feel?

❋ DAILY ACT OF FRIENDSHIP ❋

Practice showing kindness toward someone younger
than you: a sibling or cousin, a kid on the bus,
or a kid in your neighborhood.

Time-Tested Friendship

Test everything that is said. Hold on to what is good.
1 THESSALONIANS 5:21

The doorbell rang. As Sarah ran to open it, she saw her best friend Allie through the windowpane and smiled. But her smile faded as she opened the door and noticed her friend's red eyes and tearstained face. "Allie, what's wrong?"

Allie looked at the ground, her breath shuddering out. "We're moving."

"Oh, no," Sarah said, pulling Allie in for a hug. She blinked hard, feeling tears start to pool in her own eyes. She was sad, but she was also angry. How could this possibly be happening? And what would they do now?

Living across the street from each other, the two girls had been inseparable for more than a year. Sarah was worried that with Allie moving, the distance would mean losing her best friend. She knew she would still see Allie sometimes, but it wouldn't be as often.

As moving day approached, Sarah became determined to keep her friendship with Allie a priority. She begged her mom to let them hang out as much as possible. And even though they sometimes only saw each other once every other month after the move, Allie and Sarah have managed to keep in touch. They're still best friends.

The Bible reminds us to hold on to the good. It's important to hold on to what we believe but also to hold on to good friendships. Sarah's experience helped her realize that some friendships require work, but it's worth it in the end. Like Sarah, we should "hold on to the good" in our friendships by being persistent, even if we face obstacles. If someone is a good friend to you, make it a priority to spend time with them. Though distance or circumstances may interfere, intentionally connecting with a friend as often as you can may make all the difference. In the end, the hard work of friendship is worth it in order to have a friendship that lasts.

Things to Think About

When distance or other obstacles arise in friendships, what actions could you take to help maintain the friendship?

How has someone else shown persistence in their friendship with you?

❄ DAILY ACT OF FRIENDSHIP ❄

Make a list of the friendships you'd like to prioritize. Come up with a plan of action for making those friendships a priority.

Friendship in Action

Here are some simple ways to encourage a friend who is moving away:

- Send her an encouraging note in the mail.
- Text her to let her know you're praying for her.
- Call to check in and see how she's doing.
- Send a care package to her new address with some of her favorite treats.

Stand Up for One Another

KENDRA

> Dear children, let's not merely say that we love each
> other; let us show the truth by our actions.
>
> 1 JOHN 3:18

"I'm going to try out for the cheerleading team!" Terri exclaimed to her older sister Katie after the first day of school.

It was a big deal for Terri to step outside of her comfort zone and try out, even though she was shy and a bit insecure. Terri made the squad and loved cheering, but as the season went on, some of the older girls began to criticize Terri's skills and question if she should even be a part of the squad. One evening, Terri went home in tears.

Terri dropped her bag in the entryway and trudged up the stairs. She could hear music coming from Katie's room. When Terri entered, Katie looked up from her bed where she was studying. "What's wrong?"

Seeing the sympathy on Katie's face made Terri want to cry. "Everything," Terri responded as Katie handed her a tissue.

Terri sat on Katie's bed and told her the whole situation—what the other girls had said, the way they looked at her, how she felt—all of it. Katie listened, and then with a resolute look told Terri she would talk to one of the girls on the cheerleading team. Terri listened as Katie called the other girl and kindly but firmly asked her what was happening, and then explained how the way they were treating Terri wasn't right. As Terri listened, she felt encouraged that her sister would defend her.

We all need to have someone we know is going to be on our side no matter what happens—a friend who will encourage us, build us up, and stand up for us when others are being unkind. Have you ever considered that you could be that person in someone else's life? The Bible tells us we shouldn't just *say* we love each other. We should show it by our actions. It can take courage to stand up for a friend who is being hurt, made fun of, or called names, but when we do so, we are putting our love into action.

Things to Think About

Do you have a sibling, close relative, or friend who has stood up for you? What difference did it or does it make for you?

Have you had the opportunity to stand up for a friend? What happened as a result?

❀ DAILY ACT OF FRIENDSHIP ❀

Make a plan for how you will stand up for a sibling or friend who needs to know you are for them.

Do You Know Jesus?

JULIE

I am the good shepherd;
I know my own sheep, and they know me.
JOHN 10:14

"Do you know Harper?" Evelyn said to Camila at lunch, eager to inform her best friend about the new girl she met at camp. "She plays basketball too."

"No, I don't think I've run into her during basketball season. I wonder what team she is on." Camila zipped open her lunch bag. "What's she like?"

"Harper's great! She has three older siblings, and she loves horses and drawing." Evelyn paused to think before continuing. "She has a superfat, orange cat named Peanut. I really want you to meet her!"

"That's cool," Camila said. "I'm up for meeting her. She sounds nice."

In this conversation, it's easy to see that Evelyn *knows* Harper while Camila just knows a few things *about* Harper, right? She knows only the details Evelyn shared and can't say that she is friends with Harper, even if she hopes someday to be Harper's friend.

When you think about Jesus, are you like Evelyn or are you like Camila? If your relationship with Jesus is based only on what you hear in Sunday school or from a friend, you are like Camila. You know *about* Jesus, but you don't *know* Jesus. If you've asked Jesus to forgive your sins, invited him to be your Savior, and pray and read the Bible, then you are like Evelyn because you talk to Jesus directly.

Just as we build friendships over time and by doing things together, we build our relationship with Jesus the same way. We spend time reading our Bibles and ask Jesus to show us how to live our lives by reading about his. We talk to him—out loud, in our thoughts, or a mix of both—before we go to sleep and as we go about our daily tasks. We worship him when we hum or sing a favorite worship song to him.

John reminds us that knowing *about* Jesus will never be enough. Jesus wants to be our very best friend, and that only happens when we spend time talking to him and reading what he had to say.

Things to Think About

Where do you get most of your information about Jesus? Do you get it only from other people or by reading the Bible and talking to him?

Ask an adult you love how she or he talks with God and consider which suggestions you might adopt.

❄ DAILY ACT OF FRIENDSHIP ❄

Set aside ten minutes each day for reading your Bible and five minutes for talking out loud to Jesus, not in formal prayer, but as you would talk to a trusted friend.

Friendship in Action

A Secret Space: Did you know many people have a special spot where they meet with Jesus? Use your imagination to find a small place where you can hide away from distractions with your Bible and a journal to simply talk with God. It might be a favorite chair, a branch of your favorite tree in the backyard, or a small space in your closet. Use your imagination to make it perfect for you, maybe by including your favorite verses taped to the wall or your favorite blanket to snuggle into as you read and pray.

Don't Try to Guess

KENDRA

Now, dear brothers and sisters,
one final thing. Fix your thoughts on
what is true, and honorable, and right, and pure,
and lovely, and admirable. Think about things
that are excellent and worthy of praise.

PHILIPPIANS 4:8

In Brooklyn's class, her teacher lets the students pick their seat each day at tables scattered throughout the classroom. The only rule is that once the kids have chosen their spots, they have to stay there the rest of the day and can't change again until the following morning.

One day, the friends Brooklyn usually sits with filled a table and Brooklyn was left to sit at another table, by herself. To make matters worse, the three girls sitting together kept looking at her, then turning around, leaning in, and whispering.

Brooklyn began to wonder if they were talking about her. "It didn't feel good," she told her mom later. "It felt personal."

Her mom listened. Once Brooklyn had finished, she asked, "Do you think it was possible the girls weren't really talking about you?"

"I'm not sure," Brooklyn said.

Looking back, Brooklyn wished she'd had the boldness to talk to the girls and find out what they were saying. She promised herself that the next time it happened, she wouldn't try to guess, but would find out for sure before assuming the worst.

Insecurity often rears its ugly head, especially when we find ourselves alone, like Brooklyn did. The enemy loves to lie to us and try to tell us negative things about ourselves, anything to discourage us. But we always have a choice. Scripture tells us that we are to fix our minds on things that are true and lovely and right. When we feel insecure in our friendships, wondering if others are for us or not, we can focus on remembering things about our friends that are true and kind. We deserve to feel confident in our friendships and believe the best of one another.

Things to Think About

When was a time when you felt alone or insecure? How did you handle it?

What would happen if you chose to focus on what you know to be true, rather than on what you imagine your friends are thinking and feeling about you?

What are three characteristics about yourself that are true and lovely?

❀ DAILY ACT OF FRIENDSHIP ❀

When you feel insecure about a friendship, choose to talk with your friend about it.

The Smell of Happiness

JULIE

> Whatever is good and perfect is a gift coming
> down to us from God our Father, who created
> all the lights in the heavens. He never changes
> or casts a shifting shadow.
>
> JAMES 1:17

On a whim, Jaclyn grabbed a bag of hyacinth bulbs and turned to her aunt. "I saw a really cool video about getting bulbs to bloom in the middle of winter. Do you think we can try it?"

"Oh! I love hyacinths," her aunt said. "They smell better than tulips and can be white, purple, or pink." Her aunt patted her niece on the back as Jaclyn placed the bulbs in the cart.

One sunny afternoon in late December, Jaclyn pulled the bulbs out of the veggie drawer of the garage refrigerator where she'd been storing them. "I'm so excited to try this," Jaclyn said as she and her aunt set out their supplies on the kitchen counter.

"I brought these tiny bud vases that will hold one bulb each," her aunt said. "I thought you might like to give them to your friends."

Jaclyn gently placed a bulb on the top of each bud vase, allowing the bottom of the bulb to just barely kiss the water before lining them up on top of the windowsill above the kitchen sink. It didn't take long before the bulbs started shooting up the first hints of green, followed by narrow leaves, and after several weeks, tiny flower stalks began appearing.

As each hyacinth bulb began to flower, Jaclyn asked God who should get that flower and then delivered it to her friend. With each one, she included a little note in which she wrote a verse and three things she admired about her friend.

Isn't it fun to give our friends gifts that make them happy? It's one of my favorite things. Did you know that God also gives gifts? James tells us that all the good things in our life are gifts from God. That means that God sends all the things that make you happy! Isn't that an incredible thought?

Things to Think About

What homemade gifts have you received from friends?

Make a list of craft or art projects you could create to share with your friends. What supplies do you need? Do you need help from an adult you love?

❈ DAILY ACT OF FRIENDSHIP ❈

Buy hyacinth, tulip, or daffodil bulbs in the fall and force them to bloom in the winter so you can give them away as gifts. Or choose another craft project to make as gifts!

Friendship in Action

How to force bulbs: Buy a package of hyacinth, daffodil, or tulip bulbs in the fall and put them in your refrigerator until December or January. Fill small vases or jars half full of pretty rocks or marbles and add water until the rocks are only partly in the water. Snuggle your bulbs into the rocks so they are barely touching the water. Place your vase in a sunny window, making sure to keep the water barely touching the base of the bulb. You can expect your bulbs to root, grow, and eventually blossom in four to six weeks! When they are ready, give your flower vases to friends with a special note.

Little Miss Perfect

To you who are willing to listen, I say,
love your enemies! Do good to those who hate you.

LUKE 6:27

"Oh no, not Taylor," Hailey scoffed to the girl standing next to her. "She's Little Miss Perfect."

From across the locker room, Taylor froze. She had just finished changing out of her gym clothes and was about to leave. But as Hailey's words echoed off the lockers, she stopped in her tracks, her heart pounding.

From Hailey's tone, Taylor could tell her words weren't a compliment. Conversations in the room died down as the other girls looked over at Taylor—but she couldn't think of anything to say. After seconds that felt like hours, Hailey waved her hand dismissively and left the room with her friend, laughter in their wake.

The conversations started up again as Taylor awkwardly bent down, pretending to tie her shoe. Inside, she was confused. She and Hailey weren't friends, exactly, but they weren't enemies either. Taylor always tried hard to be nice to others, and Hailey's unexpected words felt like a punch to the gut. But even as she straightened up and left the room for her next class, she remembered what her dad always said when other people's actions didn't make sense: *You never know what their home life is like.*

Sometimes people hurt others because they are having a hard time with something or feel pain inside. The truth is that people don't do or say unkind things because of you. They do them because of themselves.

The Bible tells us to love our enemies. Just like Taylor, we may feel attacked when we least expect it. As Christians, how should we respond? We can start by remembering that the person's actions might be caused by reasons we don't understand. We can also watch our responses. Even though Taylor was speechless in the moment, she also didn't say anything she would regret. When we're faced with a situation where someone is being unkind, we can choose our words or our silence wisely to show love even to our enemies.

Things to Think About

Why do you think Taylor's dad reminded her that someone's home life or circumstances may be the source of their unkind words or actions?

We can't control how someone acts toward us, but we can control how we respond. Write out a list of ideas for how you might choose to respond when someone says something unkind.

❋ DAILY ACT OF FRIENDSHIP ❋

If someone says something unkind to you today, respond with patient silence or kindness rather than retaliating with mean words of your own.

A Shared Lunch

JULIE

> A generous person will prosper;
> whoever refreshes others will be refreshed.
> PROVERBS 11:25, NIV

"Oh, rats!" Teresa exclaimed as she peered into her locker, looking for her lunch box. She remembered it sitting on the hallway table at home, forgotten when she set it down to put on her shoes.

"What's wrong, Teresa?" Elizabeth Rose asked as she turned from shutting her locker. "Why do you look so sad? We're about to have lunch—the best part of the day!"

"My lunch box. It's at home, and I can't eat today's school lunch because I'm allergic to eggs and wheat." Teresa's eyes welled up with tears as she realized she would have nothing to eat and a long afternoon ahead of her.

Elizabeth Rose wrapped an arm around her shoulders. "We've got you covered. We'll share ours with you. Come on, let's go."

Elizabeth Rose is a take charge kind of girl. At her suggestion, Teresa's friends dug through their lunches, looking to see what items they had that were both egg- and wheat-free. Soon Teresa had more than enough for lunch as all the girls at her table happily offered her tidbits that she could eat.

Isn't it amazing how a dreaded situation can be flipped upside down and inside out by a simple act of generosity? Teresa's bad day was completely reversed by Elizabeth Rose's kindness and her inviting others to participate in taking care of Teresa. What was going to be a no-good, terrible day became a fun memory for all the girls who participated. Scripture teaches us that when we bless others, we are often blessed at the same time. Elizabeth Rose and the girls who came to Teresa's rescue all had more than enough to eat, and lunch that day was one of the most fun of the year.

Things to Think About

What small acts of kindness have you done for a friend that resulted in your being blessed back in return?

Ask an adult you love the same question and compare your experiences.

❄ DAILY ACT OF FRIENDSHIP ❄

Look for ways to bless your friends, and make sure to note how God blesses you in return.

Friendship in Action

Choose one kind thing to do at school this week:

- Let someone go in front of you in line.
- Smile at everyone you see.
- Help a friend who is struggling with their homework.
- Compliment three friends.
- Tell a teacher you appreciate them and why.
- Share a joke with a friend.
- Invite someone to sit with you at lunch.

Using Social Media for Good

KENDRA

> Sometimes [our tongue] praises our Lord and
> Father, and sometimes it curses those who
> have been made in the image of God.
> JAMES 3:9

As Laura walked into school, she saw students huddled together and whispering and laughing while she walked by.

"Laura!" Her friend Kara rushed up to her, grabbed her by the arm, and dragged her to the side of the hall. "Look at this!" Kara pulled up a popular social media site on her phone, showing Laura a meme of her with mean words written across the photo.

Laura's face burned. Had all her friends been laughing at this picture?

A young man she'd considered a good friend had posted the cruel image. With tears running down her cheeks, Laura texted her mom, telling her what had happened. Later that morning, her mom picked up Laura and her brother for lunch with their dad.

"You know," her dad said, "I would never treat your mom that way because I would never want to hurt her feelings. If someone is calling you names, that's not showing respect toward you." Then, making sure her brother was listening too, he said to both of them, "See how sad your sister is right now? You should never make another person feel that way. How we treat each other matters."

Laura never did receive an apology from the boy, but she was able to put it behind her, telling herself that she would not cause another person the kind of pain she'd experienced.

We can use our words to curse others or bless them. When we remember that everyone is made in the image of God, that should cause us to pause and think about the things we say before we say them. Asking, "Would I like it if someone did or said this about me?" is often all it takes to stop us from hurting people. We should be girls who use our words to compliment and encourage and pray for and rejoice with others. Let's be girls who choose our words wisely, even on social media.

Things to Think About

When did someone say or do something to you that wasn't kind? How did you handle the situation?

Who do you know who has been mistreated, and how could you support them? What could you say to bless them instead?

❋ DAILY ACT OF FRIENDSHIP ❋

Pick someone nearby in your home or school and lift them up with a compliment or word of encouragement.

Keep Your Eyes Open

JULIE

> Do to others whatever you would like them
> to do to you. This is the essence of all that is
> taught in the law and the prophets.
> MATTHEW 7:12

"Mom! Maddy and I have five classes together!" Lizzie squealed, running into the kitchen. She dropped her schoolbag on the floor as she hugged her mom.

"I guess you had a good first day of middle school, then?" Lizzie's mom said, laughing.

Lizzie nodded. Her new school was much bigger than her elementary school had been. She'd prayed to have homeroom and lunch with some of her friends. So having five of her seven classes with Maddy was beyond what she had hoped for.

"You know, honey," Lizzie's mom reminded her, "you and Maddy being together is wonderful, but don't forget to invite other girls to join you for lunch. Don't be so busy being happy together that you exclude others."

Two girls Lizzie had seen that day popped into her mind right away. Now that she thought about it, both girls had looked nervous and lonely. "Thanks, Mom," she said. "Tomorrow sounds like a great day to make some new friends. I'm going to call Maddy and let her know the plan."

It's always exciting to have one of your best friends in your classes and in your extracurricular activities, but sometimes it can be a bad thing. When we get distracted by hanging out only with the friends we already have, we might miss the fact that there are other girls who would love to be included. The Bible reminds us to be mindful of those around us—treating them as we would hope to be treated if the roles were reversed. If you are blessed with a good friend to hang out with, take time also to look for girls who are by themselves.

Things to Think About

Remember a time when you didn't have a friend in class, at camp, in dance, soccer, or church. What was it like to not know anyone else in the room?

Remember a time when someone invited you to join their group. What did she say when she invited you? How did it make you feel?

❊ DAILY ACT OF FRIENDSHIP ❊

The next time you and your friend are in an activity
or class together, agree ahead of time to include
at least one other girl in your group.

Friendship in Action

Memorize a favorite quote or verse on friendship. Here are a few ideas to get you started: Ecclesiastes 4:9; 1 Corinthians 10:24; and John 15:12.

Remember the Feeling

KRISTIN

> Do to others as you would like them to do to you.
> LUKE 6:31

Evie's hands shook as she clicked her mom's name on her cell phone. As soon as her mom picked up, the words burst out. "Mom, Kaylee wasn't nice today," Evie said, beginning to cry.

Her mom listened as Evie told her how Kaylee had invited a friend over after school and made sure Evie knew she wasn't invited.

"And then she ignored me at lunch and on the bus," Evie continued. "It really hurt my feelings."

Her mom told her how sorry she was. "Friends shouldn't treat each other that way," she said. "And I know from personal experience how much it stinks to be left out." But she ended by telling Evie something that surprised her. "Remember this feeling," her mom said. "Remember how you feel right now and how you wouldn't want anyone else to ever feel like this. So even though I know how inclusive and loving your heart is, remember this and do everything you can to make sure your actions don't cause anyone else to feel this way."

When the Bible reminds us to treat others the way we would like to be treated, it's easy to list the positive ways we'd like to interact with our friends—with kindness, love, and respect. But it's equally important to consider the unkind behaviors we've experienced in our friendships, because knowing how we *don't* want to be treated helps us choose our words and actions more wisely to avoid causing harm. In friendship, remembering negative moments can give us empathy for others who may find themselves in a similar situation. When Evie's mom asked her to remember the hurt, it wasn't just a reminder for Evie to think about her bruised heart but to seek to treat others with grace and kindness because of what she experienced.

Things to Think About

What experiences with friends do you think it's important for you to remember?

How can positive and negative experiences in friendship help us respond better in the future?

❀ DAILY ACT OF FRIENDSHIP ❀

Write down three things you've learned—
good or bad—through friendships.

You Can Do It!

KENDRA

Encourage each other and build each other up,
just as you are already doing.
1 THESSALONIANS 5:11

"I'm so excited to perform!" Eva told her mom. She winced as her mom pulled her hair into a tight bun. Eva was new to the dance team, but she'd spent countless hours perfecting her dance. Today was the day of the big competition.

"You're gonna do great, honey," Eva's mom said, patting a little blush on Eva's cheeks. "You're ready for it!"

At the convention center, Eva quickly put on her costume, then went backstage with her coach and her team to wait their turn. From behind the thick, black curtain, she could hear the other girls performing. Then she turned to her teammate Brynn and noticed that her eyes were wide and fearful.

"What's wrong?" Eva asked.

"I'm so nervous I'll mess up!" Brynn confessed.

Eva immediately grasped Brynn's hand. "You'll be fine," she told her. "We're going to do a good job."

Brynn nodded as Eva continued to hold hands with her until it was their turn to perform. As they walked onstage, Eva gave her hand one final squeeze right before they took their places.

We all can get nervous or afraid from time to time, and we need friends who will notice and encourage us in those times. And when we keep our eyes open and hearts sensitive to those around us, we'll notice—just as Eva did—that something is wrong even when our friends haven't said anything aloud yet. The Bible tells us that we should build each other up, finding ways to call out our friends' strengths and cheer them on when they are uncertain. It's what good friends do for one another.

Things to Think About

Have you ever noticed one of your friends was nervous or afraid? What did you do or say to encourage them?

How has someone comforted you when you were afraid?

❋ DAILY ACT OF FRIENDSHIP ❋

Look for someone who may be afraid or nervous and offer them words of support.

Friendship in Action

Host a talent show. Invite your friends over, then brainstorm ideas: skits, a dance or cheerleading routine, a physical talent like doing cartwheels or Hula-Hooping, singing or lip-synching a song. Practice your individual or group routines, then perform them for one another, cheering each other on.

Calling Out the Lies

> When [Satan] lies, he speaks his native language,
> for he is a liar and the father of lies.
> JOHN 8:44, NIV

"I've decided not to try out for the school play. I can't act as well as Bailey, and I can't dance. Besides, it's a musical, and I sound like a hoarse frog."

Rachel read over Khalila's early morning text as she munched her waffle. It was clear Khalila was panicking over the tryouts that afternoon after school.

Rachel quickly typed a response. "That's not true. I've heard you sing a million times. You have a great voice. You can dance. And there is more than one part, so Bailey can't play all the roles."

As Rachel reread Khalila's message, she started to get mad at the lies her friend was believing. At lunch that day, she pulled Khalila aside. "Don't believe those lies, Khalila," she gently told her friend. "You can sing and dance better than you are remembering." Rachel's words brought balance back and gave Khalila the freedom to rethink some of her destructive thoughts.

Satan's lies are difficult to detect when they are mixed with a grain of truth. He will pick on an aspect of ourselves we already feel insecure about, using those truth/lie combinations to keep us from trying out for activities or from attempting something new that might be a little hard at first. He wants us to feel like we are no-good losers instead of young women of God who can do hard things.

Sometimes, God sends a friend to remind us of the truth when we are believing lies. Rachel was that kind of friend to Khalila, wasn't she?

At other times, God asks us to be the one who tells the truth to our friend. We should be girls who are constantly alert for Satan's lies, ready to speak God's truth.

Things to Think About

How does Satan try to trick you into believing lies? Are you able to see a pattern in how he lies to you?

Ask an adult who loves you how Satan tries to trick her or him into believing lies. Is there a pattern in the lies they believe?

❋ DAILY ACT OF FRIENDSHIP ❋

Ask God if there is someone in your life believing
a truth/lie combo and then invite her over
for a hangout and a long chat.

Invite Someone Along

KRISTIN

> Don't be selfish; don't try to impress others. Be humble,
> thinking of others as better than yourselves.
> PHILIPPIANS 2:3

"Does Maren want to go too?" Stella asked Emerson. "I don't want anyone to be left out."

The two girls had spent the summer morning playing at Emerson's house and decided to ride their bikes over to Stella's home for the afternoon. They were busy searching in the mudroom for Emerson's unicorn bike helmet when Stella asked if Emerson's little sister Maren might want to go with them.

"Sure," Emerson agreed. Attaching the front strap of her helmet, she turned to holler up the stairs. "Maren, do you want to go with us?" she asked.

"Yes! Just a second," Maren said. She clattered down the stairs, feet thumping as she raced to slide on her flip-flops and catch up with the two older girls.

Can you imagine how Jesus must have felt watching the two older girls wanting to include the younger one? Philippians reminds us to be unselfish and think about the needs of others instead of focusing on ourselves or trying to impress. The two older girls didn't have to include a little sister. Because Maren was upstairs, they could have easily slipped quietly out of the house, no one the wiser. Instead, they genuinely wanted to be friendly and kind. Their actions were a reminder that the love and care we show for others in our friendships is a reflection of our character. When we model the love and grace Jesus showed, it's evident to those who are listening and watching from the outside as well.

Things to Think About

Think of a time when you were included in an unexpected way. How did it make you feel?

What are some ways you could include someone you normally don't hang out with in your regular activities?

❀ DAILY ACT OF FRIENDSHIP ❀

The next time you spend time with a friend, intentionally ask someone else (such as an older or younger sibling or a neighbor) if he or she would also like to play with the two of you.

Friendship in Action

Make a list of ten fun activities a younger neighbor, cousin, sibling, or kid on the school bus would love to do with you. Ideas could include chalking fun pictures on the sidewalk, playing tag, building a fort, riding bikes, going on a scavenger hunt that you create, or playing dolls or LEGOs. Let him or her pick from the list and then do that activity together.

Put-Ups Instead of Put-Downs

KENDRA

Gentle words are a tree of life;
a deceitful tongue crushes the spirit.

PROVERBS 15:4

"I really like your shoes," Carrie said to a passing girl as she and her friend Sabrina walked down the hallway at school.

"Thanks!" the girl responded with a smile.

Sabrina and Carrie smiled back.

"I'm trying to be better about saying something kind to others when I see something I like," Carrie explained as they walked into their next class.

"That's such a good idea," Sabrina said. She had noticed how Carrie had lately been sincerely calling out things that she likes about other girls—whether a personality trait, a kind act someone did, or even just a pair of cute shoes. *I want to do that too*, Sabrina decided.

Speaking kind words over others is a habit we should practice with all the girls we come into contact with on a daily basis. We can invest in lifting each other up rather than putting each other down—it's a beautiful thing to see!

Put-downs can be discouraging or even hurt another person's feelings. They are like deceitful words that crush the spirit, not only of the person who hears them, but of the person who speaks them in haste or anger as well. We usually end up feeling worse about ourselves when we speak angry or mean words to another. But the opposite is true too. "Put-ups" are encouraging words we can offer to others around us. They are gentle words, offering life not only to those who hear them, but to the person who is offering the words to another. We often feel better when we can offer someone some encouragement or even a compliment. Choosing our words carefully is always best.

Things to Think About

Who among your friends is really good at offering others put-ups instead of put-downs? How can you follow their example?

Who do you know that could really use a put-up?

❊ DAILY ACT OF FRIENDSHIP ❊

Look for someone that you can offer
a put-up to instead of a put-down.

Having Jesus as Your Bestie

JULIE

> Remain in me, and I will remain in you. For a branch
> cannot produce fruit if it is severed from the vine, and
> you cannot be fruitful unless you remain in me.
>
> JOHN 15:4

Alexa excitedly opened the letter from the school district, confident she was about to receive great news. Because she planned to be a surgeon someday, she had applied to take the honors science class offered at her school and was waiting to hear if she got in. As her eyes skimmed the letter, her heart clenched in despair. Tears filled her eyes. She hadn't been selected.

What do we do when the image we've created for ourselves based on our skills or talents gets ripped away from us? Have you ever been disappointed when you didn't make the basketball team or didn't get a role in the musical? In those times, we need to be careful not to mix up what we can do with who we are. Jesus invites us to find our identity—who we really are, not what we do—in him. When we understand that difference, we see that we are Jesus-followers who also happen to be bookworms, athletes, artists, and musicians. When we don't get into the class or don't make the team, it might make us sad, but it won't confuse us as to who or what we are.

Did you know that Jesus wants to be the one we turn to first in times of sadness? He would be our best friend, if we asked. He wants us to seek his advice, turn to him when our heart is broken, to read and obey Scripture even when no one else does. He is the friend who never disappoints us and who stands beside us when life doesn't turn out like we wanted.

How do we become best friends with Jesus? We remain in him, just like a branch stays connected to a vine. This means we talk to him, we read our Bible so we can learn how to follow what he taught, and we thank him for taking care of us. We trust him and consider him our best friend.

Things to Think About

How are you sometimes mixing up what you can do with who you are?

How can you start depending on Jesus like you would a best friend?

❀ DAILY ACT OF FRIENDSHIP ❀

Ask Jesus to be your closest friend and start spending five minutes journaling every day. Make lists of things you are grateful for and lists of what you are praying for.

Friendship in Action

Create your own prayer journal. Gather a plain notebook, stickers, markers, paint, and anything else you might need. Personalize the journal by writing a Bible verse you love on the cover. If you like, add some flowers and flourishes too! Use this journal to write down what you'd like to say to Jesus every day, including telling him about your friendships. Don't forget that you can use it as a space to pray for both your enemies and your friends.

Reevaluating Friendships

KRISTIN

The prudent carefully consider their steps.
PROVERBS 14:15

It took a while for Sadie to find a true, lasting friendship. At first, she was friends with Mila, but Mila always seemed to have some kind of drama going on that revolved around boys, and her attitude and words were usually negative. Next she met Ruby, who seemed much more positive, but within just a few months she began acting jealous of any time Sadie spent with other people.

"I don't know what to do," she moaned to her grandma after school one day. "I don't want to be alone, but I also don't want to be part of constant negativity and jealousy."

"Good friends can be hard to find," her grandma said. "Just keep being friendly toward others and keep a lookout for someone who might be a good friend. It's okay if it takes time."

Sadie was still kind to Mila and Ruby, but she decided that she wouldn't close herself off to other friendships. And it wasn't until she bumped into Emily that she found a true friend. Emily was upbeat, and her faith in God helped bolster Sadie's faith. When they were together, they spent hours laughing and being silly. Unlike the negative interactions she had with Mila and Ruby, Sadie and Emily had a positive, easy relationship. Though she remained friendly toward the other girls, over time her friendship with them diminished and her friendship with Emily became stronger.

When we make new friends, we can sometimes feel like we're being disloyal toward our other friends. Yet Proverbs tells us we should think carefully about the choices we make. That's true for major decisions like what job to work or who we should marry. But it's equally important to be wise in the small stuff too. Our friends have a major effect on the way we see situations and other people, how we feel about school or activities, and even how we respond to God. There's nothing wrong with taking time to consider and pray about whether a friendship that once seemed like a good fit no longer is. While some friends may last a season and others a lifetime, if we rely on God to direct our steps, we can be at peace with the friendship decisions we make.

Things to Think About

What do you think it means to be wise in our friendships? Why is it so important to be careful in friendship in the same way we're thoughtful about other areas of life?

Have you ever drifted from a friendship because it was no longer a good fit or because you had different paths? What new friends has God brought into your life?

❋ DAILY ACT OF FRIENDSHIP ❋

Write out a list of your five closest friends.
Then, write out three traits that characterize each of them.
Consider whether these characteristics are positive or negative.

Don't Do Life Alone

Come to me, all you who are weary and burdened,
and I will give you rest.
MATTHEW 11:28, NIV

"It's been months now," Mia said. "I don't know why I feel so sad all the time."

Mia's teacher, Mrs. Sampson, nodded sympathetically. "I've had a time in my life when I felt sad too." She went on to explain, "What you're experiencing, Mia, is normal. A lot of people have times of sadness or even depression."

After they talked, Mrs. Sampson told Mia she was going to call her mom, just so she knew about their conversation. Mia agreed that would be a good idea.

When Mia got home that day, she and her mom sat on Mia's bed together. Once again, Mia explained some of the sad feelings she had been having lately.

"I think it might be good for you to talk with a professional about it," Mia's mom said, giving her a squeeze.

Through a referral from her school, Mia began to meet weekly with a counselor over several months. Through those conversations, Mia began to sort through her thoughts and emotions with a trusted adult who could guide her until she began to feel better about life.

Sometimes we can feel shame if we are in a season when we are sad or down, but we don't have to feel bad about what we are going through. That is the time to reach out to a trusted adult and let them know what we are experiencing. And you know what? When we do, we'll find we're not alone. God gave us other people and himself to help us through life.

None of us are meant to do life alone. Jesus tells us we can come to him if we're worried and burdened, and he'll give us rest. He wants to be there for us when we're happy and when we're sad.

Things to Think About

When have you experienced a time you felt sad? What helped you feel better?

Make a list of adults you could talk to if you ever experience deep sadness again.

❀ DAILY ACT OF FRIENDSHIP ❀

Think of a friend you could comfort who might be feeling worried or sad.

Friendship in Action

Walk around your school or neighborhood with a friend and leave encouraging notes for others in chalk on the sidewalk.

No Means No

JULIE

Since God chose you to be the holy people he loves,
you must clothe yourselves with tenderhearted mercy,
kindness, humility, gentleness, and patience.

COLOSSIANS 3:12

"Jada Grace, can you please come in here?"

Jada knew her mom wasn't happy. She only used her full name when Jada was in trouble. As Jada walked into the living room and saw her mom looking through Jada's phone text messages, she knew why.

While Jada and her friend Amara had been having a sleepover, they had sent funny video messages to their friend Isabella. "Please stop!" Isabella had asked, over and over. She was at a family event and didn't want her phone buzzing with notifications.

Jada squirmed. She and Amara had kept sending messages and videos, telling Isabella they were spamming her. They were having fun—well, she and Amara were, anyway.

"Honey, I know you thought you were being funny and silly last night, but can you see that it was unkind to Isabella? She repeatedly asked you to stop, but you didn't listen. Remember our conversations about how no means no?"

As Jada reread the conversation, she realized that Isabella had been increasingly irritated when she and Amara wouldn't stop. Jada felt bad. She had made a mistake and owed Isabella an apology.

Sometimes we aren't very good about stopping when someone says no. We have a tendency to ignore someone's request, especially when we think the situation is funny. The thing is, we can't truly see into someone's mind or heart to understand how our words or actions are affecting them. So when someone asks us to stop, we must respect their request. Because we belong to Jesus, he expects us to be kind, humble, gentle, and patient with those around us. Respecting when someone says no is an important part of living the kind of life that pleases Jesus.

Things to Think About

How do you feel when someone ignores your "no"?

Whose "no" do you sometimes ignore? A sibling? A friend? What happens when you don't stop?

❋ DAILY ACT OF FRIENDSHIP ❋

When someone says no, stop. If you aren't sure why they are asking you to stop, kindly ask why so you can understand what was upsetting to them.

Neighbors and Friends

The whole law can be summed up in this one
command: "Love your neighbor as yourself."
GALATIANS 5:14

"Let's have a neighborhood movie night," Noelle's dad suggested.

Noelle's ears perked up. She and her family live in Minnesota where the cold, snowy months can seem like they'll never end. When spring finally arrives, neighbors she's barely seen in months start coming outside to mow their lawns and plant flowers, and summer isn't far behind.

Noelle loves spending hours outside on those long, sunny days. Sometimes she only comes inside when she's hungry. Otherwise, she's too busy running through the sprinkler with Finley, playing with her sisters and Selah in a blow-up pool, riding her bike over to Meredith's, and creating elaborate games on the swing set in the backyard with Lily. And after a long winter, it was finally nice enough outside to do all those things.

"We'll host the movie next Saturday," Noelle's dad continued, getting more excited about his idea.

Noelle felt excited too. She quickly ran over to Finley's house to tell her the news. "Hey," she said when Finley opened the door. She took deep breaths, winded from running over. "We're doing a movie night! Can you come?"

As Finley ran inside to ask her parents, Noelle started to think about what kind of snacks they could have and what movie they should watch.

The following Saturday, Noelle's dad put up a huge blow-up projector screen on the street in between their house and Finley's house. As the sun dropped further to the horizon and darkness and mosquitoes crept in, kids and adults propped up striped lawn chairs and brought popcorn and chocolates to share.

There are a number of times in the Bible where we are reminded to love our neighbors as much as we love ourselves. That doesn't just include our "neighbor" next to us in class or the person who sits in the bus seat across from us—it also includes our literal, next-door neighbors. There are all kinds of ways you can show love to them—whether it's inviting them over, watching their pets, or just talking with them whenever you see them. Through positive relationships in our neighborhood, we can demonstrate the love of Christ and gain new friends.

Things to Think About

Do you have neighbors who are friends? Why or why not?

Who in your neighborhood might be in need of a friend?

❋ DAILY ACT OF FRIENDSHIP ❋

Come up with a list of fun ways for you or your family to bless or include your neighbors.

Friendship in Action

Draw a map of your neighborhood, labeling each neighbor's house if you know their names. Then choose a kind act or way to connect with each nearby neighbor, learning their names if you don't already know them. Here are some ideas to get you started:

- Paint rocks with friends to place around your neighborhood or in a family's yard or garden.
- Ask a parent for a trash bag and some protective gloves. Go on a walk around your neighborhood with a friend and safely pick up and discard trash.
- Invite your neighbors over for a bonfire with your family.
- Host a neighborhood bingo or movie night.

God Is a Comforting Friend

KENDRA

God has not given us a spirit of fear and timidity,
but of power, love, and self-discipline.
2 TIMOTHY 1:7

When Naomi was a young girl, she was very afraid of the dark and would often have nightmares. Each time she would wake afraid in the middle of the night, she would build up the courage to leave her warm bed and run to her parents' room for comfort and security.

"Dad, can you pray for me?" she'd whisper, as tears fell from her eyes.

"Of course, honey," he'd say, and give her a hug.

Her dad was always quick to quiet her fears. He'd walk her back to her room and tuck her into bed. As he did, he would pray over her the same Scripture verse, reminding Naomi that God has not given her a spirit of fear, but of power, love, and self-discipline. He would tell her that God was her protector and friend. He would remind her that she could call on him and Jesus would be there for her.

As she grew older, Naomi started to repeat the verse her dad had spoken to her over the years. Any time she was afraid, like when she had to take speech class in middle school or when she wanted to try out for the school play, she would tell herself the truth of God's love and power in her life and heart. Naomi started to see God as her friend—someone she could go to on her own, even if her parents weren't around. She confidently knew that he would be there for her to offer the same comfort and security she had first felt from her dad.

It may or may not be a new idea to us, that God wants to be our friend, but it is true. He is a comforting one, meeting us in the middle of our fears or insecurity with his love and power to face the situation.

God wants us to turn to him no matter what we are facing, and he will always be ready to offer us his peace.

Things to Think About

Have you thought about God being a friend to you before? How have you noticed his friendship to you?

Do you go to God when you need comfort and courage? Why or why not?

❃ DAILY ACT OF FRIENDSHIP ❃

Thank God for the ways he's been a friend to you.

Praying for Others

Bless those who curse you.
Pray for those who hurt you.
LUKE 6:28

"Aunt Amy, I don't think Rose wants to be my friend anymore, and I don't think I want to bother trying to be her friend, either," Keira huffed as she walked through the front door.

"I was just heading to the kitchen for hot cocoa. Why don't we chat while we drink some?" Keira's aunt said.

As Keira sipped her hot cocoa, she told Aunt Amy the story. Lately, Rose rarely wanted to hang out, and when she did, she got frustrated easily.

Aunt Amy set her mug down thoughtfully. "Rose's dad is a soldier, and he left two months ago on a yearlong deployment. You knew that, right? Do you think maybe Rose's behavior is partly because she misses her dad and is struggling?"

Keira was quiet for a moment. "I hadn't thought about that. I know how close she is with her dad. Maybe she misses him and it just spills out in different ways. Maybe I need to give her grace."

Like Keira, we might wonder how we can be a good friend when someone is going through a really hard time—especially if it is causing them to treat us unkindly.

First, we can stop to think about a situation through our friend's point of view instead of our point of view. Some people want to be left alone when they are sad, and we shouldn't decide they don't like us just because they don't want to hang out.

Second, we can give them grace. When we are stressed, angry, sad, or scared, we might get frustrated or angry easily. It doesn't make the behavior okay, but maybe we can understand why people act that way.

Third, we can pray. Jesus loves everyone, even if they don't know him. Jesus specifically tells us to pray for the people who are mean to us and who hurt our feelings. Why? Because Jesus knows that hurt people have a tendency to hurt others. He can see the pain in their heart while we just see their bad behavior.

Things to Think About

Has there been a time when you've been sad or angry and were unkind to your friends? How did that make you feel inside?

Think of a time when a friend tried to cheer you up when you were sad. What did she say or do that helped you feel better?

❀ DAILY ACT OF FRIENDSHIP ❀

Do you have a classmate or friend struggling in some way that shows up in unkind behaviors? Pray for him or her every day for one month and find small ways to be kind.

Friendship in Action

Create a care package for a friend who is sick or going through a hard time. Pick a few of your friend's favorite items to put together in a gift bag (these do not have to be expensive!). Suggestions: a favorite candy/snack, nail polish, book, game, magazine, flower, lotion, notebook, or anything else you think they'd like.

A Needed Break

KRISTIN

> The righteous choose their friends carefully, but
> the way of the wicked leads them astray.
> PROVERBS 12:26, NIV

Sophie didn't know where things had gone wrong in her friendship with Emma. Whatever the reason, as the days marched from winter into spring, the occasional hard moments between the two girls became an almost daily occurrence. Sophie couldn't understand why her best friend was suddenly glaring at her across the room, telling other kids not to play with her at recess, and talking to classmates about why she was such a terrible person.

Sophie wanted to make peace with Emma, but Emma didn't seem to want to move on from her anger. Sophie couldn't bear the thought of a friendship failing, especially since she didn't know why things had gotten so bad. But no matter how hard she tried, she couldn't seem to smooth things over with Emma.

Later that day, Sophie's teacher, Mr. Johnson, pulled her aside to talk about the problem.

"It seems like you and Emma have been having a hard time lately," Mr. Johnson said.

Sophie nodded, blinking away tears.

"Sophie, sometimes friendships can become toxic—meaning that the harder you try to make it work, the more the friendship ends up hurting you," Mr. Johnson said. He paused, then gently continued, "I don't think you should feel you have to stay friends with Emma out of loyalty."

While Sophie was sad to lose her friendship, she also felt relieved. If you have ever been in a situation like hers, you can choose to step back as well. The Bible teaches us that the righteous carefully think about who they should be friends with—and even though we should forgive others for the pain they've caused us, that doesn't mean we should continue to allow them to wound us going forward.

Leaving a friendship doesn't mean you are failing—some situations are just unfixable. When a friendship is no longer healthy, deciding to walk away is the right choice to make.

Things to Think About

Have you ever experienced (or are you currently experiencing) a toxic friendship? How did you handle the situation?

Have you ever been the toxic element in a friendship? What habits or attitudes might need to change so you only bring kindness and joy to the friendship?

❁ DAILY ACT OF FRIENDSHIP ❁

Consider whether or not any of your friends are toxic.
Have a conversation with a trusted adult about any
relationship that may be causing damage.

Be Who God Made You to Be

KENDRA

All of you together are Christ's body,
and each of you is a part of it.
1 CORINTHIANS 12:27

"Okay, everyone, let's play a game of Marco Polo!" Abigail said as she approached the other kids in the pool.

Tonya frowned, watching as everyone readily agreed, getting into position for the game. Tonya's older sister Abigail was an incredibly outgoing person who was able to make friends easily wherever she went, while Tonya was a shy girl who usually found just one or two friends with whom she could hang out. Just then, Tonya saw a young girl sitting alone on the edge of the pool. What was it her parents would always say? "Each style of friendship is important and needed in life. Be who God made you to be. The important thing is that you are looking for the person who needs a friend."

Tonya walked over to the girl. "Would you like to play too?" she asked. The girl nodded as Tonya took her hand and they walked toward the larger group.

No matter who we are or how we most naturally make friends, we can include others in our circles of relationships, at school, church, or in our own neighborhoods, in a way that is unique to us. It doesn't really matter if we're outgoing like Abigail and make a lot of friends at one time, or are more introverted like Tonya, seeing the needs of just one person—God will still use each of us to show his kindness and love toward others.

We were meant to complement one another. This means that although our roles may be different from one another's, no one's part is greater or more important than another. We are each a piece of Christ's body together, made uniquely, to fulfill our individual roles (and that includes friendship with others). Don't be afraid to step out with whatever personality style God has given you. Don't wish you were more like someone else around you. And don't reject the people God asks you to befriend. You may just be the best person for the job.

Things to Think About

What is your personality like? Are you more outgoing or shy?

How do you feel most comfortable making friends?

❀ DAILY ACT OF FRIENDSHIP ❀

Use your friendship style to include someone who may be feeling left out, whether it's as part of a large group or just one on one.

Friendship in Action

Stargazing: Invite a friend over on an evening when it won't be too cloudy. Print off a list of constellations for you and your friend and ask your parents if you can stay up later than usual. Set up lawn chairs in your backyard and try to find as many constellations as you can.

Reaching Out

JULIE

Kind words are like honey—sweet to the soul
and healthy for the body.
PROVERBS 16:24

"Lord, be with my friend. Heal her body and take away her pain. Be close to her and give her peace as she waits for the doctor. Amen."

Penelope's text arrived as Kesia lay curled on her side in her hospital bed, trying to breathe through the pain. She had arrived at the ER an hour earlier, and her grandpa was sitting at her bedside as they waited together for the doctor. They suspected it was her appendix, and as Kesia reread Penelope's texted prayer, her tears almost blurred out the words.

Another text came through. "I wish I were there with you! How can I help?"

How can I help? Those four simple words felt so important in Kesia's moment of uncertainty and fear. She was putting on a brave face for her grandpa because she didn't want him to worry, but Penelope's prayer and question reminded her that she was loved by God, family, and friends. She had an entire group of people surrounding her with prayer and love. That knowledge helped her stay calm. And when Kesia was released from the hospital several hours later with her appendix still in her body and with medicine and the promise that everything would be fine, Penelope's words stayed with her.

It's hard to watch friends struggle with something hard while we wonder how to help and whether there is anything we can do that would make a difference. But Proverbs reminds us that kind words are good for us, body and soul. In those times, offering prayer and encouraging words is always a great first step. But simply asking the question, "How can I help?"—like Penelope did—is another wonderful way to respond. A heartfelt prayer and offer of help can point a friend back to Jesus. Even if there's nothing we can do about the situation in the moment, a genuine offer can be enough to bolster the spirits of a friend who is going through a difficult time.

Things to Think About

What has someone said to you in a moment of struggle that you found encouraging and helpful?

What might you say or what are some questions you could ask to show that you love and support a friend?

❋ DAILY ACT OF FRIENDSHIP ❋

Pick up a plant or small flower arrangement at the florist
(or gather flowers from your family's garden) and
surprise a friend who is having a bad week.

Twin Day

> God does not show favoritism.
> ROMANS 2:11

"Mom, I don't know who to ask to be my twin for Twin Day," Bailee moaned after school one afternoon. "Olivia and Sydney already have their outfits planned, and Mara asked Whitney today because they were twins together last year." As she finished listing all the girls who were already paired up with one another, she flopped on the couch with a huff.

Having switched from one school district to another this year, Bailee didn't know many of her classmates yet. And with Homecoming Week falling during the first few weeks of the school year, she didn't have much time to find a partner.

"Hmm," her mom said thoughtfully, looking up at the ceiling as though she'd find inspiration there. "What if you pick someone you might not have thought about yet? Maybe someone you don't sit with at lunch or someone with a quieter personality who wouldn't naturally have the courage to ask anyone?"

Head whirling, Bailee thought and thought until finally she remembered a girl named Monica who lived down the street. The next day, Bailee gathered her courage and asked Monica to partner with her for Twin Day.

"Mom, she is *so* excited! No one has ever asked her before," Bailee said when she came home.

Within twenty-four hours, Bailee's attitude changed from feeling excluded to actively finding someone to include. Twin Day came and went, but Bailee and Monica's friendship continued to grow.

The book of Romans reminds us that God doesn't play favorites—he loves all of us equally. But when we are on the "inside" or already paired up with someone for an activity or group project, it can be hard to remember that someone else may feel left out. As friends and *befrienders*, let's actively seek out those around us who are new, quiet, shy, or may have a hard time making friends. Our willingness to look beyond our immediate circle and invite others in not only shows that we care, it reflects the love Christ has for all people.

Things to Think About

When is the last time you faced a challenge in friendship? What opportunities did that challenge create?

What are some creative ways to include others when you face a situation like the one Bailee did?

❈ DAILY ACT OF FRIENDSHIP ❈

Ask God to show you someone outside your circles whom he wants you to include. Then make a plan to do so.

Friendship in Action

Brainstorm a list of creative ideas—actions, invitations, etc.— to include others.

Welcoming Friends

KENDRA

> After this I saw a vast crowd, too great to count,
> from every nation and tribe and people and language,
> standing in front of the throne and before the Lamb.
>
> REVELATION 7:9

A woman named Alima sat down next to Ruth and her mom at a barbecue their family was hosting. During the conversation, she told them that sometimes people give her funny looks. Alima came to their area as an immigrant several years ago and is now married with two little girls of her own. "It makes me sad that people would be afraid of me and my family without really knowing us," she said.

"It makes me sad too," Ruth's mom told her. "You and your family are some of our favorite people. You are loving and kindhearted, always willing to help."

Alima smiled at her gentle words.

After she left, Ruth and her mom talked more about their conversation. "Why are people afraid of them, Mom? They're such nice people. And their girls are so sweet."

Her mom agreed and then replied, "Sometimes people are afraid of things or people they're not familiar with. It doesn't make it right. But we can always be the ones to push past fear and get to know others."

The Bible tells us that in heaven, people from every nation and tribe will worship before the throne of God. What a beautiful picture! As Christians, we can model that same kind of community by befriending people who may not look like us. When we listen to someone else's experience that is different from our own, and try to put ourselves in their position, we are loving people the way that Jesus did. We don't have to be afraid of others because of how they look or dress, because of the foods they eat or don't eat, or because of the language they speak or the country they came from. Every person is made in the image of God, and people from every nation will stand before the throne of God someday. This frees us to be welcoming friends.

Things to Think About

Do you have friends from a different country or culture? What do you have in common?

Why do you think the Bible says people from every nation will stand before the throne of God?

How can we celebrate our differences with friendship?

❀ DAILY ACT OF FRIENDSHIP ❀

Extend friendship to someone
from a different country or culture.

Learning to Support Our Friends

JULIE

> Blessed are those who mourn,
> for they will be comforted.
> MATTHEW 5:4, NIV

"Oh, Lord. I miss Katrina so much. And I know her sisters do too. Why did she have to die?" Julia paused for a long moment. "Jesus, please help me be a good friend to Katrina's younger sisters. Amen."

Julia and Katrina first met when they were in the same homeroom three years earlier. They became close friends, and these months since Katrina died had been really hard and confusing for Julia. Julia knew it was even worse for Krista and Kennedy, Katrina's twin sisters one grade younger than her and Katrina.

Julia didn't know how to be a good friend to Krista and Kennedy as they grieved, so she asked Ms. Johnson, the school counselor, for help. Ms. Johnson helped her realize that grief is like the ocean—sometimes the water is as still as glass, and in those times, Julia could laugh until her sides ached over funny memories. Other times, grief is like huge, crashing waves that knock you down and drag you out to sea, and in those times she might sob because she missed Katrina so much.

Did you know that God will use us to comfort our friends when they lose someone they love, even if we also are grieving? We can pray for them, listen to them talk without judgment, and give them space when they need it.

As we help our friends, it's important to remember that everyone reacts differently in grief, and that's okay. Julia, Krista, and Kennedy made a pact that when one of them wants to talk about Katrina, they will let her talk and not try to change the topic or avoid the conversation if someone starts crying. It's healthy to talk about the people we miss, even if it's hard.

Things to Think About

Who are adults you love who you can turn to for advice when one of your friends loses a pet, a grandparent, a sibling, or a close friend?

Ask an adult you love what kinds of words or thoughtful actions from friends helped them when they were grieving and what kinds of words or actions didn't help, so you know things you can do and things you should avoid.

❋ DAILY ACT OF FRIENDSHIP ❋

When a friend is grieving, tell them you are willing
to listen if they ever want to tell you about their
loved one. If they don't, that's okay—don't force them.
But if they do, listen carefully and ask questions so
they know you are interested and care.

Friendship in Action

Ask three adults if you can interview them about what they wish other people would say (or not say) to them when they are sad. These questions will get you started, but you can make up your own as well:

- Think of a time you were sad. What did someone say to you that made you feel better?
- Was there something someone said that made your sadness worse instead of better?
- What do you wish you had known at my age about being a good friend when your friends are sad?

A Matter of Manners

KRISTIN

> Remind them . . . to speak evil of no one,
> to avoid quarreling, to be gentle, and to show
> perfect courtesy toward all people.
> TITUS 3:1-2, ESV

A new friend invited Elaine for a sleepover at her house, and Elaine couldn't wait. As the day approached, she packed her bag, her mind running through a list of all the fun activities she and her friend Amelia might do together.

The overnight came and went, and Elaine had just as much fun as she had expected. But at school the following Monday, she found out that the evening hadn't gone as well as she thought.

"My mom said you can't come over again," Amelia said, shuffling her feet awkwardly. "She said that 'please' and 'thank you' weren't part of your vocabulary."

Elaine was embarrassed and ashamed. While she had thought about the sleepover and the activities she and her friend would engage in, she had never even considered the impression she was making on others in the home. Even though she felt thankful inside for the fun things she'd gotten to do that weekend, her seeming lack of gratitude had reflected poorly on her. Unfortunately, she was never invited over to Amelia's house again.

While Elaine knew that expressing courteous words are important, she learned the hard way just how much courtesy and manners—or the lack of them—can impact friendships. Ever since that day, she made it a practice to always respond graciously and with gratitude in all of her relationships, including in her friendships with others.

The words we say—or don't say—matter. As Christians and as friends, we should always try our best to be kind and courteous toward others. When we forget to thank someone for a job well done or overlook someone's contribution to a group project or event, hurt feelings can result. When we choose to gossip or use our words as weapons to hurt someone, that can lead to the death of a friendship. But if we choose to use our words to encourage others or express gratitude, we can bolster relationships and strengthen friendships. After all, our words reveal our hearts. Let's choose to use them to do good.

Things to Think About

In what ways do you think the words we speak reflect our character to those around us?

Have you ever said (or forgotten to say) something to a friend that you later regretted? How might you change your response going forward?

❋ DAILY ACT OF FRIENDSHIP ❋

When you're sitting with your friends at lunch
or with your family at dinner, share one thing
you appreciate about each person.

On Mission in Friendship

KENDRA

> Don't let anyone think less of you because
> you are young. Be an example to all believers in
> what you say, in the way you live, in your love,
> your faith, and your purity.
>
> 1 TIMOTHY 4:12

Jasmine and her friend Lizzie wanted to raise money for people in need, and they recruited their brothers to help as well. They found a local program that discreetly gave kids a bag of food for the weekend if they otherwise might not have anything to eat while not at school. But what could the two friends and their siblings do to support the program?

Their parents were having a book booth at a local women's conference. "Maybe we could make magnets to raise money for the food program," Jasmine suggested. "We could sell them at our moms' book booth!"

"That's a great idea!" Lizzie agreed.

The week of the conference, they all got together one night to make posters explaining what they were raising money for, who it would benefit, and why it was important. They also discussed how they would talk about it at the conference and prepared answers ahead of time.

On the day of the conference, the kids arrived with the magnets, excited and a bit nervous to share at the booth. But it wasn't too long before they realized that talking about their project was actually pretty fun. They spent the next two days meeting new people and having conversations about helping others in their community. It felt good to share the experience with friends. Jasmine said, "I probably wouldn't have been as confident alone, but having a friend helped me not be so shy."

When we do things together with friends, we gain boldness we might not have all alone. The kids felt confident because they worked as a group, and in turn, they were an example to the women who came to the conference. They demonstrated what it means to live out what you believe by showing compassion and taking care of the needs of someone else. Don't ever let your age limit you! If you have a passion to help or serve other people, don't be afraid to do it and invite your friends to join you.

Things to Think About

What group of people are you passionate about helping or serving?

What could you do to help and who could you invite to join you?

❃ DAILY ACT OF FRIENDSHIP ❃

Ask a friend to join you in doing an action
that helps someone else.

Friendship in Action

Search out a need in your local community and then pull together a group of your friends to help meet that need. Ask a parent if you need help scheduling a volunteer day or picking up supplies.

Choosing Friendship over Stuff

JULIE

> Whatever you do, whether in word or deed,
> do it all in the name of the Lord Jesus,
> giving thanks to God the Father through him.
> COLOSSIANS 3:17, NIV

"Whoa, what?" Avery squealed as she started jumping up and down. Lights flashed on her arcade game, announcing that she had just won the five hundred-ticket jackpot. Her shouts of "I won, I won!" could be heard throughout the venue as she did a little dance of excitement.

Avery and Josie were at the arcade to celebrate Josie's birthday. As Josie exited the bathroom, she saw Avery dancing. She knew something awesome had happened. "What's going on? What did you win?" Josie asked as she reached Avery's side. When Avery told her, Josie said, "That's great! Let's go shopping!"

Five hundred tickets was more than double what either Josie or Avery had already earned. As they walked around the store, Avery could tell Josie was trying hard to be happy for her but was struggling. The item Josie wanted was two hundred points more than she had to spend, and it was hard to find something within her point total. Avery quietly double-checked her own point total and then picked out something that left two hundred points to share with Josie.

"Here, Josie," Avery said as she handed the extra points to Josie.

"Really? Thank you!" Josie gave Avery a hug.

"Of course. It's your birthday. Happy birthday, friend."

When we win a prize or receive something no one else has, it feels good, doesn't it? And it's normal that our first instinct is to keep it for ourselves. But choosing to share our unexpected blessing with a friend is a beautiful example of what Paul is talking about in Colossians when he tells us to do everything we do in the name of Jesus. God asks us to make our words and actions count for him—to reveal his love for the world, and to thank him for blessing us with good things by sharing them with others.

Things to Think About

Think of a time when someone shared their unexpected blessing with you. How did that change your day? How did you react?

How has God blessed you in ways you could share with others?

❋ DAILY ACT OF FRIENDSHIP ❋

Choose to share one of your blessings with a friend.

What We Have in Common

KRISTIN

Accept each other just as Christ has accepted you
so that God will be given glory.

ROMANS 15:7

"Mom, we're basically twins," Elise's voice bubbled from the backseat of the car. "We both like pink, unicorns, and *Dork Diaries*. We have *so much* in common!"

Just a few hours earlier, Elise had been feeling a little differently. Elise had joined Girl Scouts a few weeks earlier, two months later than everyone else. As the newest member of the troop, she was excited to join, but felt anxious about what the other girls—who had the benefit of several meetings together already—would think about her. Would they have things to talk about?

Now, driving home, Elise realized she'd been worried for no reason. Each of the girls had spent time talking about themselves in order to find out what interests they shared. She was excited to realize she and some of the other girls were much more similar than she originally thought.

When it comes to friendship, it can be easy to focus on what we don't have in common instead of what we do. Our hair or clothes may look different, our personalities may be different, or we may have different interests that appeal to us. Of course, we want to celebrate what makes us unique—but sometimes, we can use our differences as an excuse not to seek friendship with others.

If our friends are Christians, we'll always have our faith in Jesus as something to build a friendship on. The Bible reminds us that we should accept each other just like Christ accepted us. But even if someone doesn't believe the same things we do, we can focus on what we *do* have in common. When we focus on the characteristics or interests that bring us together rather than the ones that separate us, we often may find—as Elise did—that we have more in common than we thought we did.

Things to Think About

Have you ever dismissed a potential friend as someone too "different" from you, only to find out later that you actually had a lot in common with that person? Have you ever been dismissed in that way?

What do you think it means to accept others the way that Christ has accepted us?

❅ DAILY ACT OF FRIENDSHIP ❅

Make a list of all the things you have in common with
a friend. Tell that person why you're glad you have
those characteristics or interests in common.

Friendship in Action

Host a friendship scavenger hunt to find out what you have in common with others. Choose a time and location—during lunch, at recess, or on the weekend—and find friends or acquaintances to join you. For the hunt, prepare ahead of time a sheet of ten to twenty different categories to search for. Here are some ideas to get you started:

- A friend who has a sister
- A friend who has stayed in a hotel
- A friend who likes running
- A friend whose favorite color is blue
- A friend who loves cats
- A friend who enjoys green beans
- A friend who plays soccer
- A friend who has gone camping
- A friend who likes to read
- A friend who has her own room

During the hunt, mingle with your friends, ask them about themselves, and try to find a different name to write down in each of the categories you have listed.

Choose Wisely

KENDRA

If you are wise and understand God's ways,
prove it by living an honorable life, doing good
works with the humility that comes from wisdom.
JAMES 3:13

Betsy is a sixth grader, trying her best to navigate middle school. She's a good student who is tenderhearted and gets along well with others, which has made her well liked by teachers and students alike. She just has one weakness in relationships: she leans toward pleasing others.

One day Betsy felt a nudge during a math test. One of the popular girls in her class was looking at her. "Do you know the answer to question ten?" she quietly whispered.

Betsy looked around, unsure what to do. "It's ten," she whispered back, feeling guilty even while she did it.

"Betsy." Mrs. Ames stood beside the two girls' desks. "I'm afraid I'm going to have to take your quizzes. Cheating means a zero in this class."

After school, Betsy tearfully relayed the day's events to her mom.

Her mom listened and gave Betsy a hug. "I know all too well what it feels like to try so hard to be liked and accepted by others," she told Betsy. "I've always struggled with a strong desire to please others. And because I know this about myself, it makes it all the more important to choose my friends wisely because I know that they will influence me."

"Next time, I'll stand up for myself," Betsy told her mom.

The Bible says that if we are wise and understand God's ways, we should show that to others by the way we live. But when we care too much about what others think, this can affect our ability to live honorably. For example, if we spend most of our time with people who are negative, mean, or unkind, we likely will end up doing and saying the same kinds of things just to please those "friends." But the opposite is true, as well. If we spend our time with people who are kind, generous, loving, and always looking to do good for others, we'll end up living that way. Although we can always be kind to everyone, we need to be wise about who we allow to influence us and our choices.

Things to Think About

Are you someone who is easily influenced by others? Why or why not?

Have you been wise to pick friends who are wise?

❈ DAILY ACT OF FRIENDSHIP ❈

Make a list of the qualities a wise friend should have and then ask God to help you be those things for your friends.

You Are Sent

JULIE

How will anyone go and tell them without being sent?
That is why the Scriptures say, "How beautiful are the
feet of messengers who bring good news!"

ROMANS 10:15

"Jesus, why did I doubt you? You can use anyone, even someone my age. And thank you for bringing me a new friend in Bahati. She is exactly who I needed." Ana whispered her prayer as she pulled her sleeping bag toward her chin, ready to get some sleep after her full first day on her missions trip.

When Ana decided to go on a missions trip with her youth group to Alaska, she didn't know God would send her a new friend as well. Bahati was traveling with her own youth group from Kentucky, and the two girls had a lot in common.

"I'm kind of nervous," Bahati had told Ana at lunch that day.

"Me too!" Ana agreed. She had secretly wondered how God could use her when so many adults assumed she was still a kid.

"You know what?" Bahati continued. "Even though I'm nervous, I love Jesus, and I know God can work through me—and through you too, Ana."

The encouragement of a new and supportive friend like Bahati was just what Ana needed. And by the end of the week, Ana found that God had used each of them in a number of ways to show Jesus' love as they helped with the skits and games they put on for children in the community.

No matter your age, you are never too young to be sent by God out into the world to bring his message. You have relationships with your peers and the ability to speak into their life that adults do not have. You understand other girls your age in ways adults cannot because they did not grow up in the same environment. You are here for such a time as this. And God has plans to use you to bring the good news to the world—starting at your lunch table, on your school bus, on the sidelines of your sports fields, and everywhere in between.

Things to Think About

Where are places God is sending you that your parents and other adults can't go?

Who among your friends needs to hear the truth about God? Who among your friends will stand beside you to share that truth?

❊ DAILY ACT OF FRIENDSHIP ❊

Pray that God would open up conversations with your friends about his love. Be brave and confident to tell them the truth when the subject comes up.

Friendship in Action

Do a faith-building activity with your friends. Here are some ideas to get you started:

- Make bookmarks for your Bible and include your favorite verse.
- Create a poster for your room with words and pictures reminding you of all the ways God loves you.
- Host a notecard-making party to create cards that you and your friends can give to others, offering prayer or encouragement before a big test.

When We Aren't Sure What to Do

KRISTIN

When I am afraid, I will put my trust in you.
PSALM 56:3

Lexi's neighbors had lived next door for six months. Lexi didn't know the family well, but she had spent time with their son and daughter. One day, her new friend whispered something to Lexi that worried her. Her friend said that her dad was hurting her brother, using a belt that left marks. Lexi's stomach twisted into knots when her friend's brother pulled the hem of his shirt up to reveal bruises on his back. Most adults treat kids well. But some adults hurt instead of help kids. Lexi knew that is called abuse, and she also knew she needed to tell someone who could help.

The next weekend, Lexi had a sleepover at Claire's house. It was there she found the courage to whisper her neighbor's story aloud. Claire listened to her story and grabbed Lexi's hand in reassurance. "We need to tell my mom," Claire said. Knowing that Claire's mom was a social worker who worked to help kids in the area, Lexi agreed.

A few minutes later, Claire's mom crouched in front of Lexi. Her eyes were serious as she thanked her for talking to her about it. She asked Lexi to tell her what the neighbor girl had said and about the marks she had noticed. "We can look into this," Claire's mom said. "No one needs to know the information came from you. Would that be okay?"

Lexi nodded, feeling relieved. She knew she had done the right thing in trusting Claire's mom.

Sometimes we are uniquely positioned to be able to help a friend who is in trouble. But facing a big problem can feel scary. As Christians, we are never alone. Jesus is always with us. He wants us to trust him with our worries, and we can always start with prayer. But when we face situations that are too big for us to handle alone, we can also turn to trusted adults whom God has placed in our life to help us.

Things to Think About

Have you ever experienced a situation that felt too big for you? Brainstorm a list of trusted adults you could talk to in a situation like that.

❄ DAILY ACT OF FRIENDSHIP ❄

Talk to a parent or trusted adult about what to do if you think a friend is being abused in some way. Write out a specific action plan that lists who you should talk to about your worries or a help line you can call.

DAY 66
A Mentoring Friendship
KENDRA

Let each generation tell its children of your mighty acts;
let them proclaim your power.
PSALM 145:4

Carrie's family was planning to host a small group of friends and their families for an at-home Bible study. "I think I'd like to do an activity with the younger kids about the story of Noah," Carrie mentioned to her mom as she showed her the kids' Bible she'd been reading.

"That sounds like a great idea," Carrie's mom said. She helped Carrie collect the supplies she would use for the morning. Carrie carefully planned her lesson and cut out all of the things she would need.

The morning of their gathering, Carrie arranged her supplies on her kitchen table. She passed out snacks when the children gathered around. Then Carrie and her brother Abram read the story of Noah and the ark from the children's Bible and answered questions the younger children had about it. Afterward, they helped each child make a rainbow out of construction paper, a reminder of the promise of God that went along with the story.

"How did it go?" Carrie's mom asked later that afternoon.

"I liked it," Carrie told her mom. "Teaching younger kids how to pray, how to listen to God and have fun while doing it, helps me learn more about who God is too."

We often learn things best by teaching others. But honestly, sometimes it can get frustrating too. When younger kids don't listen and they interrupt, or when keeping their attention is challenging, you may wonder why it's important to teach them or if it even really matters. But the Psalms tell us that each generation is meant to tell the next about

God and all he's doing. One important part of friendship is mentoring others because mentors are friends who teach us about God, answer questions we may have, and support us. You're never too young to start mentoring someone else. We can all share stories about God with others and encourage them in their lives and faith. Having a mentor and being a mentor is an important part of friendship.

Things to Think About

Who is a mentoring friend for you? What do you appreciate the most about them?

Who could you mentor?

❀ DAILY ACT OF FRIENDSHIP ❀

Be on the lookout for someone you can mentor and encourage.

Friendship in Action

Teach a friend to do something you know how to do. This could include dancing, playing soccer or another sport, cooking or sewing, playing a musical instrument, or speaking another language. The possibilities are endless!

Letting Her Go

> Trouble pursues the sinner, but
> the righteous are rewarded with good things.
> PROVERBS 13:21, NIV

"I might start eating lunch with Maria," Katy told her mom as they drove home from the grocery store.

"Oh? Did something happen with Izzy and Ayla?" her mom asked.

Katy shrugged. "Now that we've started middle school, I feel like we don't have as much in common as we used to. They've been watching videos on YouTube that make me uncomfortable and talking about sometimes hanging out with older kids who vape."

"It sounds like Izzy and Ayla are making decisions that will get them into trouble," Katy's mom said. "I'm proud of you for noticing."

Katy had known Ayla and Izzy since kindergarten, while she and Maria had just met—but Katy had a feeling she wanted to know Maria better. "Maria makes good choices," she told her mom. "And we have a lot of the same interests."

"Lunch with Maria sounds like a very wise plan. Why don't you try it this week and see how things go?"

Did you know that very few people keep the same friends for their entire lives or even for most of their life? While some twenty-five-year-olds are still best friends with someone they met in kindergarten, far more people have different sets of friends at different points in their life. We change over time, and it makes sense that our friendships might change for a variety of reasons.

Growing apart from a friend isn't necessarily a bad thing, especially if she is consistently making choices you know are wrong or dangerous.

The Bible warns us that making bad decisions repeatedly will lead to trouble while making good decisions will be rewarded. If a friend is constantly choosing actions we know are sinful and encouraging us to do the same, we need to rethink that friendship—no matter how old or young we are.

Things to Think About

Ask an adult you love about a friendship he or she lost due to a friend making unwise or unhealthy choices. How did they handle the situation?

Do you have classmates, friends, or neighbors who are starting to make bad decisions? Ask an adult you love how to handle those changing relationships.

❋ DAILY ACT OF FRIENDSHIP ❋

If you need to make a friendship change because of repeated unhealthy choices, look around for someone who is making better decisions, and start working on developing a new friendship.

Seeking God's Wisdom

KRISTIN

> If you need wisdom, ask our generous God, and
> he will give it to you. He will not rebuke you for asking.
> JAMES 1:5

When Steph was in middle school, the way she thought and felt about herself grew increasingly dark. Most people experience mood swings and go through rough patches, but when Steph's negative thoughts about herself continued to get worse, her best friends worried about her.

They urged her to talk to two mentors who hosted a weekly small group, but Steph had no desire to talk about what she was feeling. In fact, she threatened to stop being friends with them if they went against her wishes by approaching the mentors.

Eventually, though, her friends chose to do what they believed was right. Despite Steph's protests, her friends sat down with the mentors and explained what was going on. Hearing the details of how Steph had been feeling and how she'd been talking, the mentors stepped in. With their help, Steph began moving beyond the dark place she'd found herself in. As time went on and her thoughts became more positive, she was incredibly grateful her friends intervened.

Friends need to do what is right—even if it's hard. Steph's friends were worried about losing her friendship but decided her overall health and well-being were more important.

It can be difficult to know when we should stay quiet about a friend's problem or when we need to speak up about it. In the book of James, we're reminded that if we need wisdom, we can always approach God first. Though we probably will never hear him speak aloud, his Word can act as our guide, and his love and comfort are always near. When we aren't sure what to do, we can always ask for help—from God and from adults we trust. Though Steph was initially mad at her friends for bringing her truth to light, in the end, she was grateful.

Things to Think About

Have you ever been in a situation where a friend threatened to cut off your relationship if you did something they didn't like? How did you respond?

Brainstorm a list of situations where doing the right thing is more important than fearing that you may lose a friendship.

❈ DAILY ACT OF FRIENDSHIP ❈

Ask a trusted adult to help you come up with a list of signs or symptoms that can help you identify if a friend is struggling with depression, as well as an action plan for how to approach the situation if you think a friend needs help.

Friendship in Action

What's the difference between sadness and depression? Everyone feels sad sometimes, and that's normal. Usually, feeling sad is attached to something we've experienced. Depression is often when you feel sad for a long time without really knowing why. If you aren't sure if you are or a friend is depressed, talk with a counselor, doctor, or other trusted adult about your feelings.

A Good Team Captain

KENDRA

> Jesus called them together and said, "You know that
> the rulers in this world lord it over their people, and
> officials flaunt their authority over those under them.
> But among you it will be different. Whoever wants
> to be a leader among you must be your servant,
> and whoever wants to be first among you must be
> the slave of everyone else."
>
> MARK 10:42-44

Lola was chosen by her coach to be one of two team captains for her school's softball team. Her coach told her they picked her because she was such a good friend to everyone on the team. She was honored to be chosen but also felt a little insecure about the position. *Will they accept me as the captain or criticize me?*

That afternoon she found her dad sitting at the kitchen island and asked him what he thought.

"I think it's a good thing, as long as you know what it is to be a good captain," her dad said.

"What do you mean?" she asked.

"Well, let's talk about what makes a good leader."

As they talked, Lola noticed that the qualities of a good leader were also the qualities of a good friend: a good leader 1) cheerleads and encourages others; 2) listens compassionately and helps those who struggle; 3) thinks about how others feel; and 4) understands that the team as a whole is stronger than the individual parts. A good leader doesn't 1) criticize, belittle, or make fun of others; 2) talk about teammates behind their backs; 3) ignore those needing help; or 4) refuse to listen to others' concerns.

Lola and her dad discussed all these points, and then he said, "Being a leader, just like being a friend, really isn't about you, but about the people you are serving. I think you'll make a great captain because you are kind and loving and willing to help others."

We can all show the traits of a good leader and friend, whether we are a team captain or not. As girls who love Jesus, we are asked to be an example of him to others. We can be the first to exhibit the characteristics of a leader who serves those around her well.

Things to Think About

Have you ever thought of yourself as a leader? Why or why not?

Which of the traits of a good leader listed earlier in this devotion do you do well? What would you like to continue to work on?

❋ DAILY ACT OF FRIENDSHIP ❋

Be the leader and friend God designed you to be by picking one of the good traits from this devotion and offering that to the friends around you.

Obey the Nudge

JULIE

For the rest of you, dear brothers and sisters,
never get tired of doing good.

2 THESSALONIANS 3:13

"Can I pray for you in any way?" Kate texted.

Her message arrived early one morning when Scarlett was feeling particularly sad. Kate always seemed to sense when things weren't quite right. Her notes were often perfectly timed to arrive just before Scarlett had to face something hard. Scarlett smiled through tears as she read Kate's message, loving both her and Jesus at that moment. It wasn't surprising that Kate almost seemed like a mind reader. She always seemed to listen to God's nudging and to be particularly gifted at reaching out in compassion and care to those around her. Her perfectly timed notes reminded her friends that they were not alone, that God sees them, and that he loves them so much that he nudges their friend Kate to reach out.

Isn't someone like Kate a wonderful friend to have? We can all learn from Kate. How? We start by asking God to nudge us with a thought when he wants us to check on a friend. When we listen to that thought or little voice in our head, we'll be amazed to later find that our action was perfectly timed.

Being God's representatives is important, but sometimes our chance to obey is short. If we put it off, we may forget to do it. We don't want to get so distracted by our daily tasks that we ignore when we are asked to encourage our friends with a little note or text message. Obeying God's nudge allows God to bless others through us, serving as his representatives in the lives around us. It requires listening to that still, small voice in our heart and then being willing to set aside time out of our busy days to obey. It is always worth it.

Things to Think About

Who in your life is good at reaching out with encouraging notes or texts?

What are some fun ways you can reach out to others with encouragement?

❋ DAILY ACT OF FRIENDSHIP ❋

Make a list of people in your life who might need someone praying for them and send them an encouraging note.

Friendship in Action

Buy a few spring flowers, potting soil, and clay pots at a local garden center. Paint the clay pots with acrylic paint and let them dry overnight. Plant a flower in each pot, filling in with the potting soil as needed, and then give them away to teachers, neighbors, your pastor, or anyone else you think needs a day brightener.

First Impressions

KRISTIN

Sensible people control their temper;
they earn respect by overlooking wrongs.
PROVERBS 19:11

Standing on the risers, Robyn sang quietly as she waited for the fourth-grade concert rehearsal to begin.

A new classmate turned toward her, a frown on her face. "Your voice is ugly," she said.

Robyn was focused on the upcoming concert, and she liked her voice, so she didn't let the girl's rudeness bother her. She kept on singing.

A couple of days later, the choir was rehearsing for the concert again when Robyn noticed the same girl fiddling with the neckline of her concert costume. The Velcro wasn't sticking. It kept rubbing up against her lower neck and irritating her skin. Noticing the problem, Robyn reached out and folded the Velcro over so it stuck to the costume material. The girl turned around, smiled, and said, "Thanks!" After a pause, she continued more thoughtfully: "I like you."

When someone says or does something unkind—especially if we don't know them well—it can be hard to give them the benefit of the doubt. Yet if we respond with anger or defensiveness, we may only fuel an argument or gain an enemy. Robyn's story reminds us that we can't rely on first impressions to give us a true reading of someone's character. People are imperfect, but when we are gracious in the midst of their weaknesses and still show kindness despite their shortcomings, we can make a difference—and we might even make a friend.

Proverbs tells us that when we control our temper or overlook wrongs, it reflects well on our character. When we choose to respond with kindness, we may find that our second interaction with someone is much better than the first. Our decision to respond with grace (or, in Robyn's case, to not respond at all) reflects our merciful, loving God, who has graciously forgiven us and given us the second chance we need too.

Things to Think About

How do you react when people say or do unkind things to you? Do you respond with anger or with kindness?

How does the way we choose to respond to others reflect our own heart?

❀ DAILY ACT OF FRIENDSHIP ❀

Think of someone who has hurt you and give them a second chance by reaching out in kindness.

Chase Your Own Dreams

KENDRA

This is my commandment:
Love each other in the same way I have loved you.

JOHN 15:12

"You ready, kid?" Sara's dad stood by the door, keys to the family van in hand.

Sara nodded, tightening the laces on her brother's old soccer cleats. Both of her brothers played soccer, and after practicing with them at home for several months, she knew she really wanted to try out for the travel team in her community. The only thing was, she wasn't sure she wanted to try out for the soccer team alone—but none of her friends had wanted to try out with her.

"I'm proud of you for trying, Sara, no matter what happens," her dad said as they drove into the lot where the tryouts were held.

The morning went better than she thought it would. She loved being on the field. The next week, she was so excited to find out she'd made the team! And several weeks later, at the first game of the season, a few of her friends stood on the sidelines cheering her on, happy that she was doing something she loved.

There may be times when you, like Sara, are interested in things that your friends are not. Remember that it's perfectly okay to pursue what you are passionate about. Each of us should be free to go after what we're good at—academics, sports, music, clubs, drama—or any other activity available to us. Good friends will encourage you to chase your dreams and cheer you on, just like you should encourage them even when they are interested in things that are different from you. The Bible says we are to love one another the way God has loved us. One way we can do that is by supporting our friends' activities and interests, rejoicing with them when they succeed.

Things to Think About

What activities do you enjoy? Are they different from your friends' favorites?

How can you support a friend in a dream she is following?

❋ DAILY ACT OF FRIENDSHIP ❋

Offer some encouragement to a friend who
is pursuing a dream of their own.

Friendship in Action

Plan a friend get-together where you each create your own "dream" boards of things you like to do, favorite Bible verses, hopes for future jobs or school. You can use markers, paint, pictures, magazine cutouts, or whatever you like—the more creative, the better!

Being Trustworthy

> A gossip goes around telling secrets, but
> those who are trustworthy can keep a confidence.
> PROVERBS 11:13

"Did you hear that Nisa got a D on the math test?" Even as the words were leaving Mei Hau's mouth, she knew she had made a mistake.

Ugh! Why did I say that? Mei Hau wished she could rewind the last ten seconds of her life. She hadn't meant to tell the group of girls at the lunch table about the low grade her friend had gotten on the test. The words had just slipped out as they were talking about how hard Mr. Smith was as a math teacher and how challenging his tests were. Mei Hau felt terrible. She had exposed her friend's weakness in math to others who weren't even her friends.

It's too easy to share information that isn't flattering or kind, even if it is the truth. Many girls thoughtlessly do this all the time, probably without really considering their words. Our culture tells us that if something is true, it's okay to share. But that's not how Jesus wants us to act.

It is important to guard our tongues and not expose the hard parts of our friends' stories to teasing or mockery. If we've been entrusted with information that makes a friend vulnerable, we need to guard that information and protect her by not sharing it.* A good way to determine whether or not you should share something is to ask yourself the following questions:

---

* Unless a friend shares the kind of information that should not be kept secret. See day four for more on how to navigate that kind of situation.

Is it true?

Is it kind?

Is it necessary?

If the answer is no to one or more of those questions, you should most likely not share. Proverbs reminds us that the best policy is to let people share their own stories—that way we won't accidentally reveal something hurtful. By contrast, asking questions and genuinely listening to another's story is a great way to start a conversation, and it's a great way to learn something new about the people around you.

Things to Think About

Has someone ever shared information about you that you wish hadn't been shared? Did you continue to trust her with personal information?

Think of a time you shared information you shouldn't have. How do you think the other girl may have felt?

❈ DAILY ACT OF FRIENDSHIP ❈

Instead of telling a story about another person,
practice asking questions that invite those around
you to tell their stories. Oftentimes, people love
to share their stories if you express interest.

Tears at the School Dance

Love each other with genuine affection, and
take delight in honoring each other.
ROMANS 12:10

"Have fun tonight, honey! I'll pick you up at nine," Leah's mom called out as her daughter opened the car door, hopping down onto the concrete sidewalk.

"Thanks, Mom!" she said. Up ahead, she could see her friends Teresa and Kristina at the entrance to the school. The sixth-grade dance was about to begin.

As the bass music thumped and light glittered from the disco ball hung high in the gymnasium, Leah saw another friend, Stefanie, hurry from the room with tears in her eyes. Leah just wanted to keep dancing and chatting with Teresa and Kristina, but Stefanie needed her. Leaving the gym, she hurried to catch up to find out how she could help.

As she suspected, Stefanie's tears were over girl drama: a friendship had gone sour. As she hugged and comforted Stefanie, Leah thought how much she was grateful to have friends who never used their words to tear her down.

Sometimes friendships bring us to tears. We can never completely stay clear of pain, but choosing our friends wisely can help cut down on some of life's drama. When we choose to treat others with the same love and compassion that Jesus has shown us, we become safe friends. Safe friendships are ones in which friends treat each other with kindness and respect. Safe friends don't talk about us behind our backs; they are honest and trustworthy. Safe friends don't leave other friends out or try to make us choose one friend over another. Instead, they work to include others and treat everyone with honor. When misunderstandings happen, safe friends believe the best about us, tell us they are sorry, and choose to work through the problem. Safe friends are the ones who comfort us when we feel sad or hurt.

You are unique and smart and beautiful just as you are. A safe friend will see the best in you and encourage you. And she may help you avoid most of the "sixth-grade dance tears in the bathroom." And, as a safe friend, you can do the same for her.

Things to Think About

Think about your friends—are they safe or unsafe? Can you confide in your friends, knowing they won't gossip about you to others? Do your friends speak to you with kindness, or do they cut you down or make you feel bad?

Are you a safe friend?

❇ DAILY ACT OF FRIENDSHIP ❇

Be a safe friend by encouraging or giving wise advice to your friend.

Friendship in Action

Make a playlist of songs you'd like to include in a dance party. Gather some friends or siblings and turn the music up loud.

Stand Up for Others

KENDRA

> Some people make cutting remarks, but
> the words of the wise bring healing.
> PROVERBS 12:18

"That school is so bad."

"Yeah. Only kids who get in trouble go there."

As her community-wide sports team warmed up for practice, Elena overheard kids talking about how awful one of the schools in their district was. Her heart sank as she listened, unsure what to do. They were talking about the school she attended. She knew why they were talking about her school, and she'd heard others' comments before. Her school was very diverse. Some people thought that was a problem, but Elena loved her school and the other students. She had many good friends and was hurt that others would think so poorly of them.

With a sigh, Elena finally decided that today she wanted to speak up. "I go to that school," she said.

The others looked a little embarrassed and listened as she told them one of the reasons she liked her school. They nodded with new understanding. One student even apologized, saying they didn't know.

Afterward, Elena felt good that she had stood up for her school and her friends. She knew that, at that moment, she had done the right thing. She had shared the truth honestly without anger. It made the other kids consider what they had been saying and how it might be hurtful to others.

We all make thoughtless comments from time to time. Watching what we say is important when it comes to friendship. We want to speak words that are wise and bring healing to others, not words that cut others down. A valuable trait of a friend is to be trustworthy in what we say and the way that we stand up for what is right.

Things to Think About

Have you had an experience where you had to choose to stand up for someone else? What happened?

What do you think it means to be wise with your words and not to be cutting in your remarks?

❊ DAILY ACT OF FRIENDSHIP ❊

The next time you notice someone using cutting words
to a friend or acquaintance, use your words wisely
to stand up for that person.

Only Jesus in Common

> Live in harmony with each other.
> ROMANS 12:16

"How did we become friends?" Tori laughed as Cora jumped out of her car and began walking toward Tori. "You sparkle in the morning light!"

"I know, right? Aren't these new shoes awesome?" Cora grinned as she opened Tori's car door to get in. "I'll make you into a fashionista yet. Are you nervous for your hockey game today? Thank you for inviting me, it's fun to watch you play!"

Tori and Cora are the best of friends, and they'll be the first to tell you that the only thing they have in common is Jesus. Cora loves sparkle and fashion. Tori loves hoodies and athletic wear. Cora curls her hair every day. Tori wears ponytails. Cora likes theater. Tori prefers sports. Cora adores New York City. Tori enjoys any place that has an ice rink and hockey.

Cora and Tori celebrate their differences rather than trying to force each other—or themselves—to be something they are not. It is their differences that allow them to see a situation from another perspective and have experiences they wouldn't otherwise have. Because they accept one another for who they are, their friendship is uniquely special as they find humor in their preferences (without bad intent) and learn new skills as they take turns supporting one another's hobbies and interests.

How boring the world would be if we all loved the same things, thought the same thoughts, and had the same interests! Tori and Cora are right. Finding friends who have interests and talents different than our own is a great way to see the world through someone else's perspective, especially when you both love Jesus.

Living in harmony with others doesn't mean we must be exactly alike. In fact, God made us individually unique, with varied interests and talents. When we are grown, he is going to scatter us throughout the state, the country, and world. He'll put us in places to influence people around us based on the unique way he made us. Instead of trying to blend in, let's celebrate the unique way God made us and those around us.

Things to Think About

What hobbies or interests do your friends have that are different than yours?

Who do you know that has a hobby or interest that you might like to learn more about?

❋ DAILY ACT OF FRIENDSHIP ❋

Strike up a conversation with someone you don't know well. Ask about her hobby or interest that is different than yours.

Friendship in Action

Ask a friend to make a friendship collage with you. Gather construction paper, markers, scissors, glue, and some old magazines your family doesn't mind if you cut up. Cut pictures from the magazines that represent things you each like, such as clothes, sports, books, movies, or pets. Trade half your pictures with your friend, then glue the pictures to a piece of construction paper to represent your unique friendship!

Look Deeper

KRISTIN

Look beneath the surface so you can judge correctly.
JOHN 7:24

Standing just inside the classroom door on the first day of school, Savannah hesitated as she looked around the classroom.

"Sit here," Allison said, catching her eye and motioning to the empty desk next to her. Surprised, Savannah nonetheless headed that way, offering a grateful smile to Allison as she slid into the seat. Savannah knew who Allison was, but they weren't friends. Allison was pretty, stylish, and in with the popular crowd, while Savannah had friends outside of that circle. She'd never considered Allison as a possible friend, assuming she was probably shallow and silly.

When the class ended an hour later, she gathered up her notebook and books and headed out the door.

"Savannah!" someone called. It was Allison. "Hey, want to sit together at lunch?" Allison asked, catching up to Savannah.

Although Savannah was unsure what was prompting Allison to seek her friendship, she was curious and said yes. As the girls filled their trays with French toast sticks and fruit cups and found a table, Savannah quickly realized that she and Allison had much more in common than she had thought. As long as she was judging Allison based only on her pretty face, trendy clothes, and cool group of friends, she hadn't noticed how smart and funny she was.

The Bible reminds us that we shouldn't judge by appearances because they don't tell the full story. It's only when we're willing to look beyond how someone is dressed or the way they style their hair that we can get to know who they really are, and it's only through genuine conversation that we can determine what someone else is really like inside. True wisdom is finding out who someone is before judging whether or not they would be a good friend. And sometimes—as Savannah did—we might be surprised at what we find.

Things to Think About

Have you ever judged someone and then later found out they were different than what you had expected? Why or why not?

Has anyone ever judged you without spending time to get to know you? How did you feel about that?

❈ DAILY ACT OF FRIENDSHIP ❈

Have a conversation with someone
you've seen before but never talked to.

Build Each Other Up

Don't use foul or abusive language. Let everything
you say be good and helpful, so that your words will
be an encouragement to those who hear them.
EPHESIANS 4:29

"She's not always nice to me," Isla told her dad one evening after dinner. "Sometimes she even teases me in front of others, and it kind of hurts my feelings."

Isla's dad nodded in understanding. "Do you know why George and I are such good friends?" he asked her.

Isla shook her head no.

"Because he doesn't tease me about being bald, and I don't tease him about being short. That's what good friends do. They build each other up; they don't tear one another down."

Her dad went on to explain that he and George had a shared understanding that they would never make fun of one another, and they would always be respectful of one another.

"Sometimes even adults use humor in a way that puts someone else down instead of building them up. I've decided I don't want to be that kind of friend," he said. "You know, maybe you want to talk to this friend about her comments. Maybe she doesn't realize what she's doing and that it's hurting your feelings. Maybe then she'll stop."

Isla agreed to take her dad's advice and try talking to her friend.

Friendship is something we all have to work on. When we create healthy habits early in life, they stay with us as we grow. Looking for friends who build you up rather than put you or others down—and being that kind of friend to others—is a valuable quality in friendship.

The Bible gives us the same advice Isla's dad did when it says that rather than abusing our friends or mocking them, we should speak good and helpful words that encourage others. That is the very definition of what makes a good friend. Let's work to build one another up, not tear each other down.

Things to Think About

Have you had an experience with a friend who teased you? What happened?

Do you have a good friend who encourages you? How have they built you up?

❇ DAILY ACT OF FRIENDSHIP ❇

Be specific when you encourage a friend today.
Say things like, "You did a great job at . . ." or
"I really appreciate that you . . ."

Friendship in Action

Use sticky notes to write about a quality or strength each of your friends possess and then secretly put the notes on their lockers or desks. Here are some examples: *You're really good at math. You always help others. You are a really good listener. I'm glad you're my friend.*

The Apology

*Make every effort to keep yourselves united in
the Spirit, binding yourselves together with peace.*
EPHESIANS 4:3

"Do you think Riley felt excluded?" Kelsey asked Hazel as they carried their trays to their lunch table.

Hazel nodded, feeling ashamed of the way she had acted. She and Kelsey are best friends and love to hang out together, especially when they are in a place where they don't know very many people. Hazel had invited Kelsey to the neighborhood picnic held in her backyard, and they had chosen to hang out by themselves, chatting in the huge climbing tree in her front yard and later hiding in the lilac shrubs in the backyard, even though Riley, her newish neighbor and classmate, was there too. Hazel had noticed that Riley didn't have anyone to hang out with, but that didn't stop her from hiding away with Kelsey.

Hazel knew she owed Riley an apology, so she knocked on Riley's door the next afternoon, and with sincerity and no excuses she told her how sorry she was for not including her. "Will you give me a second chance to be a better friend?" she asked. Riley accepted the apology, and both girls talked about how hard it can be to feel excluded.

"You should sit with Kelsey and me at lunch tomorrow!" Hazel said before she left.

Recognizing when we've been hurtful—even unintentionally—and being brave enough to say so is hard. That's partly because it requires us to be humble and admit that we were wrong. But Jesus wants us to be girls who bring peace and a feeling of community to those around us, not exclusion and hurt feelings. When we exclude someone, the right thing to do is to say we're sorry and make sure we do better the next time.

Things to Think About

Ask an adult you love about a time she or he had to apologize. What did they do to make it right? How did their friend respond?

Think about past apologies others have made to you—what parts worked? What parts felt insincere?

❋ DAILY ACT OF FRIENDSHIP ❋

Do you need to say you're sorry for pain you've caused?
To seek forgiveness before God?
Don't let the sun set without acting.

Friendship Bucket List

I recommend having fun, because there is
nothing better for people in this world than to eat,
drink, and enjoy life. That way they will experience
some happiness along with all the hard work
God gives them under the sun.
ECCLESIASTES 8:15

"What should we put on the bucket list this year?" Ashlyn's dad asked early one morning as she and her sisters sat crunching on toast with peanut butter and honey.

"The largest candy store!" her oldest sister crowed. The Science Museum, a play, a parade, carnival rides—the list grew as the girls brainstormed ideas.

"Ashlyn, what do you want to add to the list?" her dad asked, pen in hand.

Ashlyn thought about it for a minute. "Ice cream for breakfast," she finally said, a smile lighting her face as her sisters nodded their approval.

Every summer, Ashlyn's family comes up with a bucket list. Together, they write out a list of activities and experiences they'd like to do over the course of the summer. Then, they put the list on their refrigerator, and they spend the next three months crossing items off of it. Some of their favorite bucket list ideas have included riding roller coasters, water balloon fights, a treasure hunt, and eating breakfast in bed.

The family bucket list also helps the girls strengthen their friendships. Ashlyn's sister Noelle has asked their neighbor Finley to join them in their backyard scavenger hunt, and their mutual friend Lily has spent many hours playing Chutes and Ladders with them (a life-size version made out of chalk on the driveway). As a family, they invite friends over for a rib fest or for bonfires (including a delicious s'mores bar). Who knew that lemon marshmallows on a cinnamon graham cracker, paired with white chocolate, could be so delicious? Ashlyn was more than willing to try out each and every yummy combination.

God wants us to work hard and seek him in all we do, but he also wants us to enjoy the beautiful world he's created. We're bound to experience hard times in our friendships, but those times are balanced out by the joy and love friendship brings to us. As Christians, let's begin by thanking God for the gift of his creation. Then, let's look for ways to celebrate this life by spending time with our friends—enjoying nature, exploring new places, and looking for adventure.

Things to Think About

What's the most fun thing you've done with a friend?

What's one adventure you'd love to experience with a friend?

❋ DAILY ACT OF FRIENDSHIP ❋

Come up with a Friendship Bucket List.
Post it on your refrigerator as a reminder.

Friendship in Action

How to make a friendship bucket list:

- Brainstorm ideas with a friend—interesting places to visit in your city or state, fun foods to eat, games to play, movies to watch, ways to help others, art or projects to create, adventures that are free or inexpensive—and compile them in one list. (Make sure to check with a parent or adult to be certain the list is doable.)
- Print or write out a copy of the list for you and your friend.
- Place the list somewhere you'll see it often, such as a refrigerator or desk.

What a Friend We Have in Jesus

JULIE

> If you are filled with light, with no dark corners,
> then your whole life will be radiant,
> as though a floodlight were filling you with light.
> LUKE 11:36

Gracie prayed, "Jesus, you know my heart. And you know I hate this school year! Everyone else seems to be having lots of fun, and I'm miserable and lonely. I know smoking is bad, but if I'd tried the e-cig Trina offered, I'd fit in and have friends." Gracie wiped angry tears off her pillow as she prayed, hoping her little brother wouldn't hear her crying and come looking for her.

The next morning, Gracie decided to make Jesus her best friend. She started reading her Bible every day and talked to Jesus all the time. In the shower. When she walked the dog. And when she was doing something creative like drawing. She told him what she was afraid of, what she was worrying about, her dreams, and the mistakes she made. As Gracie got to know Jesus better, she realized that some of the YouTube videos she was watching when her parents weren't home weren't what he would want her to watch. They used bad language that she was starting to use too. Everyone else watched these videos, and she watched because she felt left out at lunch when others were talking about them and she hadn't seen them. Gracie told Jesus she was sorry and stopped watching the videos.

Have you had times in your life when you were lonely like Gracie because classmates and friends were making bad choices? Gracie made the right decision when she prayed about how she was feeling and started spending more time with Jesus. He loves us unconditionally—which means there is nothing we can ever say or do that will make him stop loving us. And because he loves us so much, he gives us guidelines so our lives will be full of the light of truth and goodness. Jesus asks us to live differently from our classmates and neighbors because he knows some of the choices people around us make lead to trouble, and he wants better for us. He wants us to avoid activities that will hurt us physically or emotionally. He is trying to protect us.

Jesus loves you so very much that, long before you were born, he died for you so that your sins would be forgiven. He is the best friend you could ever hope to have, and the guidelines he gives you are because he loves you so much.

Things to Think About

Where are your favorite places to talk to Jesus? Make a list of the times and places you are most likely to talk to Jesus and compare it to a list made by an adult who loves you.

Which of Jesus' commands are harder for you to obey? Why?

❋ DAILY ACT OF FRIENDSHIP ❋

Find a quiet place to open your Bible for ten minutes and have a chat with Jesus about everything going on in your life. Ask him to show you verses in Scripture to guide your week.

Be Excited for One Another

KENDRA

Be happy with those who are happy, and
weep with those who weep.
ROMANS 12:15

"You're different," Alisha observed one day.

"What do you mean?" her friend Eleanor asked.

"You're actually happy for me when I tell you about good things that
are happening to me."

"Of course I am! You're my friend," Eleanor replied.

"Not all girls are happy for me," Alisha said with a shrug.

Eleanor knew that it was true. Sometimes other girls didn't seem
pleased about Alisha's successes or didn't want to hear about them.
But Alisha was a good friend to Eleanor. They listened to one another,
comforted each other when they were sad, shared their thoughts and
feelings, and cheered one another on. Alisha was always sincerely glad
for Eleanor when something good was happening in her life, just like
Eleanor was for Alisha. That was one thing that made their friendship
so strong.

Sometimes our own or others' insecurities can hinder us from
being happy for those around us. Maybe we find ourselves jealous of
something a friend has, is doing, or has accomplished. It's normal to
sometimes wish we had things others have, but our response to someone else's happiness should be to rejoice with them. The Bible tells us
that we should be happy for those who are happy and cry with those
who cry. Even if we want something that someone else has received,
we can still choose to be excited for them. Jealousy is common in our
society—people often want what others have. But we don't have to live

that way. Instead, we can be glad for our friends while also trusting that God has good things for us too.

Things to Think About

Have you ever been jealous of a friend? How did you handle it?

What could you have done differently (if anything)?

❄ DAILY ACT OF FRIENDSHIP ❄

Celebrate with a friend who has had a recent success.
Bring her a cupcake and make it a party.

Friendship in Action

Celebrate someone else! If it's a friend's birthday, call them, make them cupcakes, or give them a small gift to celebrate their special day. To celebrate someone's success, cheer them on or throw a surprise party with ice cream, whipped cream, sprinkles, and toppings such as chocolate or caramel sauce for ice-cream sundaes.

Choosing Your Battles

JULIE

> I say, love your enemies! Pray for those who
> persecute you! In that way, you will be acting
> as true children of your Father in heaven.
>
> MATTHEW 5:44-45

"Mom!" Natalie rushed through the front door. "Those boys were at it again!"

After her mom listened to yet another story of Natalie and her friends facing off with a group of boys in the lunchroom, she asked, "Honey, what are you fighting for? Are you sure God is asking you to fight this battle?"

Confused, Natalie paused for a long moment before saying, "We don't like them because they are always causing trouble. Today, they were throwing food. Ugh. We are enforcing the rules."

"Hmm. Why aren't you allowing the lunchroom monitors to handle those boys? Maybe they need someone to be friendly toward them rather than picking a fight."

When Natalie paused to consider, her mom asked a follow-up question: "As a girl who loves Jesus, where is he in your fight?"

These two questions led to a crucial conversation about what it means to be a young woman who strives to reflect Christ to her classmates, discerning which battles Jesus asks her to pick and which battles he might ask her to leave unfought.

That's a tricky question, isn't it? How do we know the answer?

Sometimes Jesus asks us to reflect the love of Christ instead of fighting. This isn't always an easy thing to figure out, especially when our emotions are involved. The most important question to ask is: "Does this conflict honor God?" If not, perhaps this battle is not yours to fight. It's important to remember that we are the children of God and that we have to be wise in the battles we choose to fight. Are we loving our enemies when we pick fights with them? Could we respond differently instead of fighting?

Things to Think About

Have you been engaging in conflicts that demand your own rights or have you been defending another person's rights?

How can you approach conflict in ways that honor God?

❀ DAILY ACT OF FRIENDSHIP ❀

Ask God to show you the battles you've been
fighting that he has not asked you to fight.
Decide how to approach those conflicts with friends
and classmates in a way that honors God.

Build Each Other Up

KRISTIN

> We should help others do what is right
> and build them up in the Lord.
> ROMANS 15:2

Carisa moved around to a few different school settings when she was growing up. Because of this, she fell behind in her studies and struggled with reading. The year she was adopted, her new home brought other new environments, including a new school. Although she was naturally outgoing, she felt nervous and worried about catching up on her schoolwork and making friends at her new school.

But when Carisa met Tamara, she knew Tamara was different—in a good way. Tamara didn't make Carisa feel judged for the things she struggled with in school. Instead, her new friend supported and encouraged her. When Carisa would write out rough drafts, Tamara would read through them for her before Carisa wrote the final draft, praising her efforts and offering feedback. When Carisa slept over at her house, Tamara would read aloud to help Carisa fall asleep and feel less alone. They played video games and ate chips and salsa, spending time doing everything or nothing together. As long as they were together, they had fun.

Paul reminds us in the book of Romans that, as Christians, we should build each other up. This can take a lot of different forms. You could tell your friend you're happy to see them, help them study for a test, or work on a project together. You might compliment them on something they did well or a characteristic they have that you admire, or you might speak encouraging words to them when they're having a bad day.

Building each other up increases our faith and helps us grow spiritually. Whenever you go out of your way to build up a friend, you meet their needs in a way that is both loving and God-honoring. And when we choose to build one another up, we not only strengthen our faith, we also strengthen our friendships.

Things to Think About

Who in your life is good at building you up?

Why do you think it's important to build up our friends?

What are five ways you could build up a friend?

❋ DAILY ACT OF FRIENDSHIP ❋

Using the list you brainstormed,
choose one way you could build up a friend—then do it.

Friendship in Action

Organize a "Secret Friends" exchange with a group of friends. First, decide how long the exchange will last—a week or a month are typical. Next, each girl in the group should draw the name of another girl, keeping the name she drew a secret. Then, each day (if it's for a week) or each week (if it's a month), each friend should give or do something small and encouraging for the friend whose name they drew. At the end, reveal who your Secret Friend was!

What's in Your Heart?

KENDRA

> Whatever is in your heart determines what you
> say. A good person produces good things from the
> treasury of a good heart, and an evil person produces
> evil things from the treasury of an evil heart.
>
> MATTHEW 12:34-35

Lori wrote the mean post about her friend Mary and put it up on social media while she was still mad. "I can't believe Mary would not invite me to the beach when she asked April," she told her mom later.

"Honey," her mom replied, "I know you wished you could have gone too, but her parents told me they only had room for one friend in the vehicle."

Immediately Lori felt ashamed. She went to take down her post, but it was too late. Mary, April, and several other friends had already seen her harsh words. Lori apologized, but Mary was still hurt.

Social media can be a really good or a really bad thing, depending on how it's used. Some people use social media to build friendships, encourage others who are lonely, and share about supporting important causes and needs around the world. But others use social media to post mean things, call others names, and even threaten others. It is sad to see some of the destruction that can come from our words posted online.

Have you sometimes wondered why that is? People are often much bolder to say negative things on social media than they would be to say the same things to someone's face. It's as if not actually looking the other person in the eye, not recognizing them as a real person, somehow makes people careless about being hurtful.

As girls who love Jesus, we are called to a higher standard, remembering that whatever is in our hearts will come out of our mouths. Does this mean we'll never have mean thoughts about someone else? No. But it does mean that we can still address what is in our hearts and be careful about the words we speak—in real life and online. Many of us live by this phrase: *If I wouldn't say it to someone in real life, then I shouldn't put it out on social media.* We want to be known as girls who love Jesus and show his love and compassion to others, all coming from a good heart.

Things to Think About

Have you been in a situation where you spoke negatively about someone else online? What happened?

How can you be careful with your words when speaking with others (either in person or online)?

❀ DAILY ACT OF FRIENDSHIP ❀

When you feel ready to say something harsh
to someone else, first pause and make sure your
words aren't hurtful to the other person.

Seek Wisdom

The LORD grants wisdom!
From his mouth come knowledge and understanding.
PROVERBS 2:6

"Some of the kids in middle school are 'dating.' They usually break up after a week. It causes so much drama. Tara, my friend from choir, is telling me to date William, and I keep telling her that we are just friends. It's hard. I don't want to date in middle school, but she keeps teasing us. I'm not sure what to say to get her to stop." Eliza felt better as she wrote out her feelings in the journal she shared with her mom, knowing that her mom would read her words and think about her response before writing back.

Eliza and her mom started sharing a journal about six months ago. It's just a yellow school notebook, but they decorated it with stickers and markers. Now, they write all sorts of things in it: silly drawings, lists of their favorite foods, favorite memories, and even hard things, like Eliza telling her mom that she was being teased for not dating. They agreed that it would work to write about these things instead of talking about them face-to-face if Eliza wanted, as long as they both promised to read each other's words and pray before responding.

One of the most important things to do as you are growing up is to seek wisdom. Life can be confusing, and it's natural to have questions about building friendships, navigating school, and so many other topics. Often, our friends won't be able to give good advice about these topics because they are trying to figure it out too! But the Bible is full of wisdom that applies to friendships, school, and life in general.

A good place to start is with Jesus' teaching in the Gospels. The adults who love you can help you understand how the things Jesus says apply in the situations you are facing. Maybe you'd like to have a shared journal, like Eliza and her mom did, where you can write down the embarrassing or hard stuff. Jesus puts loving adults in our lives because he knows how hard these years can be and that we all need help as we become young adults who love him and love others. Wisdom comes from God, and he promises to give it to anyone who prays for it.

Things to Think About

How do you currently seek wisdom when life is hard or confusing? A journal? A coffee date with an adult who loves you? Talking in the car?

In what areas of your life do you currently need to seek wisdom? Friendships, boys, schoolwork, or other topics?

❋ DAILY ACT OF FRIENDSHIP ❋

Ask an adult who loves you to discuss how you are going to seek wisdom about hard friendship questions or embarrassing things. Make a plan with them so you both know what to expect.

Friendship in Action

Decorate a Wisdom Journal to share with an adult who loves you. Buy a spiral-bound notebook, pick out some fun stickers you both like, and then pull out the markers to add a favorite Bible verse and other encouraging quotes to the cover of the journal. You get to decorate the front and the other person gets to decorate the back. See who can be the most creative.

Testing the Heart

KRISTIN

Fire tests the purity of silver and gold,
but the LORD tests the heart.
PROVERBS 17:3

Mandy had good friends in elementary school, but when she transitioned to middle school, it felt like starting over. All of the students were placed into five different teams, and the only people Mandy knew on her team were boys she'd been friends with in elementary school. All of the girls were strangers.

Even though she wanted to make friends with the girls, she'd often hear them whispering about her and talking about how she was only friends with boys. Feeling excluded, Mandy decided it was easier to stay with her current friends than to try to make any new ones.

One day, a girl sat down next to Mandy in choir, tucking her feet underneath the chair. Catching Mandy's eye, she smiled. "Hi, I'm Chelsi," she said, tilting toward her. Her voice was open and friendly, and Mandy felt herself relaxing as they talked about the class teacher and assignments.

Within a few weeks, Chelsi mentioned that she'd love to hang out together, but Mandy was suspicious. She was worried that Chelsi only wanted to be friends with her in order to meet her guy friends. Mandy decided to give it time. If Chelsi seemed to truly enjoy her company, without bringing up the guy friends, Mandy would know Chelsi truly did want to be her friend.

As time passed, Mandy and Chelsi's circle of friends started to overlap, and the two girls developed a friendship that lasted many years.

When we've been hurt in the past or felt excluded, it can be hard to trust other people. We may wonder about someone else's motives or question how genuine their offer of friendship may be. But Proverbs reminds us that while fire tests and refines items like silver and gold, God tests people's hearts. Our willingness to open ourselves up to others and test their hearts (by observing how they treat other people) will ultimately give us the wisdom we need to determine if someone is truly a good friend or not.

Things to Think About

What does it mean to "test" another person's heart? How can you apply that idea to friendship?

What are some ways we can begin to trust others again after we have been hurt?

❈ DAILY ACT OF FRIENDSHIP ❈

Think of the person who has been your friend
the longest. Send them a note or message to
thank them for standing the test of time.

A Different Perspective

JULIE

*There is no longer Jew or Gentile, . . . male and
female. For you are all one in Christ Jesus.*
GALATIANS 3:28

"Where are you from?" the woman in line behind Ceena and Lynn asked.

"I'm originally from New York City, but I moved here a year ago," Ceena replied with a smile.

"No. Where are you *really* from? Your skin is too dark to be from New York," the woman asked again.

Ceena started to fidget uncomfortably. She is an American citizen who grew up in New York City. Because her parents are originally from India, Ceena is a beautiful blend of her Indian heritage and her American roots. But since Ceena looks Indian, strangers ask her crazy questions that make her feel as though she must choose between these two parts of her that are equally important. Sometimes, people even say really insulting things or make jokes about her Indian culture. It's incredibly hurtful.

Lynn had no idea Ceena's daily experiences were so very different from her own until they became friends. But because of Ceena, Lynn realized that sometimes she unintentionally asks strangers questions that make them feel like outsiders. After the woman turned away, Lynn smiled sympathetically at Ceena and resolved to draw others in with her words, rather than make them feel like they don't belong.

We can talk to strangers about a million other things that do not point out our differences and save the questions about differences until we are close friends. Finding topics to talk about that highlight similarities—at least at first—creates inclusion rather than exclusion.

Sometimes we can act exclusive in our churches too, not wanting to open our arms to people who look or act differently than we do. But Jesus tells us that his family is going to be a beautiful blend of differences—different cultures and skin tones, different ages, different interests. It's wonderful to be part of a family that welcomes everyone.

Things to Think About

Think of a time someone asked a question that made you feel excluded instead of included. What could that person have asked or said instead?

What are some ways you can welcome those around you by highlighting your similarities?

❈ DAILY ACT OF FRIENDSHIP ❈

Think carefully about the questions you ask someone when you first meet them, especially questions about culture or heritage that highlight why they are different from those around them.

Friendship in Action

Think ahead: Plan out ten questions you can ask to start a conversation focused on what you might have in common rather than on physical differences. Here are a few suggestions to get you started:

- What's your favorite after-school activity?
- Do you have a pet?
- Who is your favorite singer?
- What's one interesting thing you wish people knew about you?
- If you could have a superpower, what would it be?
- Now it's your turn! Feel free to ask a friend or family member for other ideas.

We Aren't in Competition with Each Other

KENDRA

> We are God's masterpiece. He has created us
> anew in Christ Jesus, so we can do the good
> things he planned for us long ago.
> EPHESIANS 2:10

"Race you to the finish!" Piper called over her shoulder to her friend Brynn. She looked back as Brynn's pace slowed to a jog. Piper stopped to wait until Brynn had caught up to her. "What's wrong?" she asked.

"Not everything has to be a competition," Brynn responded, kicking the dirt on the school track.

"I'm sorry," Piper said. "You're right. We can just finish together." The two friends jogged to the finish.

It happens a lot—we compete on sports fields, in classrooms, music halls, and art studios. Competing as part of a sports team or league isn't necessarily bad. It provides opportunities to encourage us or build community among people. But in God's Kingdom, we are not to see ourselves in competition with one another.

We don't compete with others for God's love or his grace. We do not have to compete over dreams that we have or gifts we've been given. God has assignments and hopes for each of us, so we don't ever need to think that another girl is our competition in our efforts to accomplish our dreams.

Just like a painting is considered a work of art and completely unique, so God views us as a masterpiece, created new in Christ, so we can each do the good things he's planned for us long ago. When we fully understand this truth, we stop seeing ourselves as in competition with other girls and are free to cheer on those around us in all they are doing.

Let's be girls who show up for one another while confidently pursuing the passions that God's given to each of us.

Things to Think About

Do you sometimes feel like you are in competition with other girls? Why or why not?

What are some interests or passions God has given you?

❈ DAILY ACT OF FRIENDSHIP ❈

Be a cheerleader for your friends by encouraging them in the unique gifting God's given them.

The Summer Camp Friendship

KRISTIN

This is my command—be strong and courageous! Do not be afraid or discouraged. For the LORD your God is with you wherever you go.
JOSHUA 1:9

"Morgan, do you want to go to Camp Shamineau this year? They have a horseback-riding camp," her mom said one day during breakfast.

Mouth full of crunchy cereal, Morgan used her time spent chewing to think about it. The pictures and description in the glossy catalog looked interesting, but she was nervous about not knowing anyone. Swallowing her fears along with her breakfast, she nodded. "Yeah, that sounds fun," she said.

As the first day arrived and she and her mom drove toward camp, Morgan's stomach fluttered with nerves. What if she didn't get along with the other girls in her cabin? What if they were already friends with other girls? As every mile brought her closer to their destination, she felt a mix of fear and excitement. She knew Jesus was with her, but she still worried about being left out or not fitting in. When they finally arrived and she settled into her cabin, she overheard the other girls in the cabin introducing themselves.

"I'm Sophia."

"I'm Brooke. Where are you from?" Brooke asked.

"Monticello," Sophia answered.

Morgan gasped. "What? I'm from Monticello too!"

"So am I," Brooke said.

As the week continued, Morgan quickly became friends with Sophia and Brooke. All three of them loved horses, and they realized that they lived just a few neighborhoods away from each other. They had traveled all the way to summer camp just to meet friends who lived at home. Between the horsemanship skills, trail riding, evening hayride, campfires, and chapel times, the days passed quickly. By the end of the week, Sophia, Brooke, and Morgan were inseparable.

In the Bible, we're reminded that we can face every day with courage because God is always with us. That promise—that he'll be with you "wherever you go"—is one that we can hold on to whenever we step out to try something new. When we face our fears in pursuit of adventures (and friendships), God's comfort and steady presence can give us the courage we need.

As the week drew to a close, Morgan was thankful she had decided to come. Not only did the things she had worried about not happen, but she was able to return home with two friends who lived close enough to keep in touch with.

Things to Think About

Have you ever tried an activity or experience that you felt worried about beforehand? Did that experience make you more or less likely to try something new in the future?

What does it mean to have God with us wherever we go?

❈ DAILY ACT OF FRIENDSHIP ❈

Be brave in pursuit of friendship by trying something new.

Friendship in Action

Brainstorm a list of organizations you'd like to investigate or activities you'd like to experience. Here are some questions to consider:

- Is there something you've always wanted to try but haven't?
- What topics or experiences interest you?
- What kind of cost is involved in the activity?
- What activity sounds like fun?
- Where would you like to volunteer?
- Would the activity fit in with your family's schedule and values?
- Do you like doing activities with other people or prefer to go solo?
- Is there an activity you could ask a friend to do with you?

Fight Fair

Do not make friends with a hot-tempered person,
do not associate with one easily angered, or
you may learn their ways and get yourself ensnared.
PROVERBS 22:24-25, NIV

"Honey, you should call Adelae and talk about this instead of texting," Zoe's aunt warned.

Adelae had accused Zoe of saying something that Zoe hadn't said, and Zoe really didn't want to talk to Adelae about it. Secretly rolling her eyes at her aunt, Zoe ignored her advice and decided it was easier to explain her side of the story over text.

Unfortunately, Adelae misunderstood Zoe's texted explanation and got even angrier. Adelae called Zoe ugly names and turned several classmates against Zoe. Zoe was brokenhearted and couldn't understand why a misunderstanding had gotten so out of control.

It's natural to get into disagreements and misunderstandings with our friends and classmates. In fact, the Bible has a lot to say about anger because it is an emotion we all feel from time to time, and Jesus knows that. He also knows how destructive anger can be when we don't deal with it correctly. Proverbs warns us to avoid people who love to argue and fight or we might adopt the same habit. Or we'll get caught up in their drama and be miserable.

There are four guidelines (I call them the Rules of Fighting Fair) for engaging in a healthy disagreement to help avoid the angry drama trap. First, never call names. Second, don't drag others into the fight, and don't ask them to pick sides. Third, never touch another person in anger. Fourth, speak to the other person *in person* or over the phone about disagreements. Don't text. Even all the emojis in the world can't communicate true emotion and tone of voice. Did you know that 80 percent of our communication comes through body language and tone of voice? Only 20 percent of our communication comes from our actual words! No wonder Zoe and Adelae ended up in a drama nightmare. Texting is one of the worst ways to resolve disagreements!

Proverbs warns us to be careful with how we communicate with our friends. If you practice "fighting fair" when you feel angry, it will help you avoid Zoe and Adelae's situation—allowing a simple misunderstanding to turn into angry drama—and will serve as a tool you can use your entire life.

Things to Think About

Which of the Rules of Fighting Fair are hardest for you to follow?

Which of the Rules of Fighting Fair are the easiest for you to follow?

❉ DAILY ACT OF FRIENDSHIP ❉

Pick one of the Rules of Fighting Fair that is harder for you
to follow and practice that new skill this week.

Too Much Talking

KRISTIN

Too much talk leads to sin.
Be sensible and keep your mouth shut.
PROVERBS 10:19

Alissa tugged Madison to the side of the hallway and whispered in her ear, "Did you hear what Lucy said about you?"

Madison's eyes widened as Alissa related the rumors she'd heard. Madison wasn't that close with Lucy, although they were friends with the same people. "I don't know why she would say that," Madison said, trying to shrug it off as she headed to her next class.

But as the day continued and more people asked her to verify the things Lucy had said, Madison felt her hurt beginning to build. Finally, she snapped. The next time someone asked, Madison bad-mouthed Lucy.

In the moment, she felt a sense of righteous anger. She hadn't done anything to Lucy. The attack had come out of nowhere. She wanted people to take her side. But as the day wore on and the drama continued, Madison began to realize that she'd reacted the wrong way. Talking badly about Lucy didn't defuse the situation or make Madison look any better. It made her look worse. As her temper cooled, guilt crept in. She wished she'd never responded the way she had, but now it was too late.

We've all experienced hurt feelings because of something said about us. And most of us have said angry words about or to someone else, often because we felt wronged. But the Bible tells us that too much talking can lead to sin! That doesn't mean it's a sin if you like talking to people. It's thoughtless talk that usually gets us in trouble.

God wants us to be gracious and kind to those with whom we

interact. The warning to "keep your mouth shut" is a reminder that we need to choose our words carefully. Rather than say things we will later regret, it's always better to err on the side of silence or kindness. Refusing to engage when people stir up arguments with us is always a better solution.

Things to Think About

Have you ever wished you'd kept your mouth shut instead of responding to someone's unkind words? What happened as a result of engaging with their attack?

What are strategies you can put in place to avoid saying things you will regret?

❃ DAILY ACT OF FRIENDSHIP ❃

If someone provokes you, refuse to respond.
If no one tries to make you angry, practice talking less
by asking a friend specific questions and listening to
her response. Consider how watching our words—
both good and bad—influences others.

Friendship in Action

Decorate a Friendship Jar using paper, glitter glue, rhinestones, or anything else you'd like. Place the jar in a location you will notice often, like on a shelf or desk in your bedroom. Any time someone does something kind for you, write it down and place it in the jar. On hard days, pull out the notes and read them to remind yourself of the good friends you have. (Someday, take the time to remind that friend how much their kindness meant to you.)

What Do You Believe about God?

KENDRA

The LORD is merciful and compassionate,
slow to get angry and filled with unfailing love.
PSALM 145:8

"I have a hard time seeing God as a loving Father since my dad is so distant," Angela admitted to her Sunday school group one morning during their discussion of God's love.

She'd been a Christian for as long as she could remember. But because of her difficult relationship with her earthly father, who is harsh and not around very much, she still sometimes wondered if God truly cared about even the small things in her life.

"I'm sorry to hear that," Mr. Johnson, the Sunday school teacher, said. "What do you hope that God is like?"

Angela played with her skirt. "Kind. And loving."

Mr. Johnson nodded. "Anyone else?"

"Forgiving," the girl next to Angela said.

"And compassionate," a boy across the table chimed in.

"Yes," Mr. Johnson agreed. "I think God is all of those things, but we have to have eyes to see those traits. This week, let's ask God to show us that he is those things."

The group nodded agreement as they prayed.

Later on that week, Angela got a call from a friend who just wanted to chat, and she was reminded of God's love. As she was reading her Bible, she came across a verse that told her God is merciful, and she smiled as she thought how true it was.

"Thank you, God, for being all these good things," she prayed. "Keep showing me more of who you are."

We all can have relationships with others that distort what we believe about God, but those things don't change the fact that God is good and loving. We don't ever have to wonder what he's really all about—we can go to his Word to discover his character. He'll never hide himself from us.

Throughout the Bible we see that God is kind, compassionate, and slow to get angry with us. His love never fails or ends. Wow! This is such good news. No matter how other people treat us, no matter if others see our value or not, whether they want to be friends or not, how God feels about us is very clear. He loves us, always. We never have to doubt that. He is the very best friend we can always rely on in this life.

Things to Think About

How do you think God feels about you? Why do you feel this way?

How has God been a good friend to you?

❀ DAILY ACT OF FRIENDSHIP ❀

Thank God for the ways he has been a good friend to you.

The Mean Girl in Our Head

JULIE

> Neither height nor depth, nor anything else in all
> creation, will be able to separate us from the love
> of God that is in Christ Jesus our Lord.
> ROMANS 8:39

*Ugh. My nose has a funny bump in the middle of it. Why did I even bother
to try out for the play—they'd never want someone so weird looking in that
role—* Crystal paused midthought as she bent closer to the mirror. "Ew.
Ew. Ew! Is that a pimple on my chin?" she murmured, utterly horrified.
I'm so gross!

"Mom!" Crystal wailed out loud, "I cannot go to school today!"

Do you have a Mean Girl in your head like Crystal has? A voice in
your head that constantly tells you all the ways you don't measure up, all
the ways in which others are better, smarter, prettier than you? Did you
know this is something many girls struggle with, even when they become
adults? We listen to the Mean Girl, accepting her poisonous comments
as true, even when people who love us tell us the opposite.

That internal Mean Girl voice is not our friend, does not tell us the
truth, and is not the voice Jesus wants us to listen to. If we pay attention
to it, that voice will stop us from doing all the things Jesus has planned
for us. It can even keep us feeling lonely and far from God, even though
Paul reminds us in Romans that there is nothing we can do and no place
we can go that will ever separate us from God's love.

How do we stop the Mean Girl voice? First, we learn to recognize
it. When you start beating yourself up mentally, pause and ask whether
you would speak those words to your best friend. If not, that's probably
your Mean Girl voice.

Second, replace those words with the words of a true friend—Jesus. If you've asked Jesus to be in charge of your life, he calls you beloved, a daughter of the King, his adopted sister—did you know that? Jesus has so much to say about you, all of it filled with the promise of a good future. Let his words fill your mind—not those of a Mean Girl.

Things to Think About

With an adult you love, each make a list of the comments your Mean Girl voices want you to believe and then compare lists. Which of your comments are similar?

Ask your adult to help you find several Scripture verses that will remind you of who and whose you are. Write them down and put them in a place where you will see them often.

❈ DAILY ACT OF FRIENDSHIP ❈

Any time your Mean Girl voice makes a comment, immediately repeat one of the Scriptures you've written down over yourself.

Friendship in Action

Invite friends to a Scripture card art night. Use blank index cards, permanent markers, and watercolor paints to create five beautiful Scripture reminders to put on your bathroom mirror, on your bedside stand, in your locker, and two other places you look at all the time.

You Can Pray for Friends

KENDRA

*We are confident that he hears us whenever
we ask for anything that pleases him.*
1 JOHN 5:14

"I know a lot of people, and I'm a part of a lot of activities," Kate admitted to her younger sister Addison one evening when Addison had biked over to see her. "But I don't have any close friends."

"But you're always with people," Addison responded as they sat together on Kate's front porch. She knew her older sister was friendly and outgoing.

"I am," Kate said. "But I'm still lonely. So I've asked God for friends. And now I've invited a few women from my church to be a part of a book club at my house."

A few weeks later, Kate told Addison on the phone that all the women she'd invited had agreed to come. Even after only a few meetings, they began to share the good and hard things happening in their lives, cheer one another on, and pray for one another. Kate's prayer had been answered. "You can ask God for friends too, Addison," she said, as they were about to finish the call.

Kate's words resonated with Addison. She asked, "Would you pray with me?"

"Of course!" Kate said.

The next day at school, Addison noticed a new girl walk into her choir class. "Hi, I'm Addison," she said to the girl. "There's a chair by me if you want it."

The girl nodded yes with a grin. As she sat down and they began to chat, Addison felt good that she had taken the advice of her sister to pray for and then actively pursue friends.

You don't have to wait until you are older to have a group of really good friends. You can ask God to help you find friends, no matter how old or young you are. God loves to answer our prayers, and he does not want us to have to go through life alone. The Bible says that if we ask for anything that pleases him, we can be confident he hears us. Just like Kate, we can pray and then be bold in taking a step of faith to make a new friend.

Things to Think About

Can you remember a time you were lonely? How did you make a new friend in that time?

Who around you may be feeling lonely that you could befriend?

❀ DAILY ACT OF FRIENDSHIP ❀

When you feel lonely, pray. Ask God to bring you a good friend. Then be on the lookout for who your new friend could be and start a conversation.

Leading with Love

KRISTIN

Do everything with love.
1 CORINTHIANS 16:14

Molly was confused. She and Andrea had been in orchestra together for a while, and Molly considered her a good friend. Yet every time she asked Andrea to spend the night at her house on Saturday nights, Andrea said no. What was baffling to Molly, though, was how Andrea always said no immediately, without ever saying she'd think about it or ask her mom.

"I don't get it," Molly told her mom one day, admitting that she didn't know why Andrea kept saying no.

"Maybe there's more to it than her not wanting to stay over," her mom reasoned. After thinking for a moment, she asked, "Do you want me to talk to Molly's mom and see if we can find a solution?"

Relieved, Molly nodded yes.

The next time the girls had an orchestra concert, Molly's mom approached Andrea's mom and gently asked about it.

"Oh, that's because Andrea knows we have temple on Saturdays," her mom said. Their Jewish traditions meant they worshiped on Saturday evenings.

"I completely understand," Molly's mom said, then paused. "I don't want to make it awkward for you, but we'd be fine with Molly going to temple with your family."

From then on, the girls alternated. If they stayed at Andrea's house, the girls went to Jewish temple with her family. If they had a sleepover at Molly's house, they went to Christian church together on Sunday morning. In this way, the two friends were able to find a solution that respected their families while still enjoying fun sleepovers together.

As friends, it can sometimes feel tricky to navigate relationships with those who don't share our beliefs, but that doesn't mean we can't extend a hand of friendship. Jesus loves everyone, and as his ambassadors here on earth, we are to show love to those around us as well. Sometimes that means simply listening or being present for a friend. Other times, it means recognizing that even though we may not believe the same things that our friends do, or even if we have different traditions, we can still find ways to honor our friends' beliefs without compromising our own. Because we have Jesus in our hearts, we take him with us everywhere we go—and this is one way we can show his love for others.

Things to Think About

What does it mean to "do everything with love"? What might that look like?

How can you respond with love to a friend who has a different rule or belief than you do?

❋ DAILY ACT OF FRIENDSHIP ❋

Ask a friend to tell you about something
in their life that's unfamiliar to you.

Friendship in Action

Brainstorm fun meal or snack ideas to make with a friend at your next sleepover, like setting up a taco bar, hosting a make-your-own-pizza night, having an ice-cream sundae bar, or creating a s'more bar.

Don't Follow the Crowd

KENDRA

> I am giving you a new commandment: Love each
> other. Just as I have loved you, you should love each
> other. Your love for one another will prove to the
> world that you are my disciples.
>
> JOHN 13:34-35

"Who's that?" two girls whispered as the new girl walked into school.

"I don't know," the other girl replied. "But her hair looks weird."

Maria frowned, listening to the unkind comments. "Hi, I'm Maria," she said, approaching the new girl. "Don't worry about those girls, they're not very nice to anyone."

"Thanks." The girl smiled shyly. "I'm Anna."

Anna had just transferred from another school in a neighboring town. For whatever reason, the popular girls at school decided they didn't like her. She was a nice girl, but still every day they bullied her— teasing her about her looks, her body, or her clothes. It was awful.

As the school year went on, things got worse as other students in that grade joined in. Their strength was in their numbers. No one in the student body challenged anyone in this large group of girls to stop. So they didn't. Sometimes even Maria felt pressured to make fun of Anna, but she knew that wouldn't be loving—so she tried to stand up for Anna instead. But even with the support of Maria, not much changed.

Many times adults at the school attempted to put a stop to the bullying, but it would only help for a few weeks before kids would start being mean again. About halfway through the year, Anna decided to transfer back to her old school. Maria was sad to see her new friend go but hoped she'd find a different school easier.

The kind of group bullying that happened with Anna is a reminder that we can all fall into a group mindset—for good or for evil. We can be swayed by the people around us. But we are called to love each other as this will prove to the watching world that we are Jesus' disciples. When we see a group being unkind to someone, we can choose to join them or we can do the right thing and choose to stand up for the person being bullied. We do not have to follow the crowd, especially when they aren't following the ways of Jesus.

Things to Think About

When have you seen a group of people do something together—whether for good (to help or encourage others) or for evil (to bully or hurt others)?

When a group is bullying someone, how can you choose to not follow the crowd and instead show other girls the love of Jesus?

❋ DAILY ACT OF FRIENDSHIP ❋

Choose to be kind to someone who often gets picked on.

Serving God Together

> Where two or three gather in my name,
> there am I with them.
> MATTHEW 18:20, NIV

"Wait, what? Your birthday party is at the animal shelter?" Breyann asked as she squinted at the birthday invite Lilah handed her.

"Isn't that cool? I didn't know it was a thing until I started volunteering there. We get to groom some of the friendlier cats, play with a few of the dogs, and cuddle with Thumper, their resident rabbit. The shelter uses it as a way to build awareness for animals who need a home." Lilah grinned as she thought of all of her friends brushing cats.

"What about cake and presents? Aren't you going to miss out on all the birthday stuff?"

Lilah's smile got even bigger. "Well, I still get cake and candles, but I talked to my foster mom and she asked if I wanted my presents to go toward the animals this year. I've thought about it, and that's what I want. See? I included a list of things the shelter needs, like catnip, dog bones, and old towels."

Sometimes our very favorite memories with friends are when we're serving God together. There is something incredible about partnering with friends to serve a meal at a homeless shelter, package emergency meals for kids halfway across the world, or create gift baskets to drop off at a women's shelter for Mother's Day. While we serve, we can pray that God would use our gifts to bless others.

Did you know that the Bible tells us that serving God together with others is powerful, and that God is in the midst of that gathering? It's true. When we serve God in a group, it is harder to be discouraged, easier to solve problems that may arise, we get more accomplished than if we were doing it alone, and it's simply more fun!

Things to Think About

Make a list of ways you and your friends can work together on a service project to bless others. What project would you choose? What supplies do you need? Who would you invite?

❀ DAILY ACT OF FRIENDSHIP ❀

Set up a service project with your friends.
Before you start, don't forget to pray for Jesus
to be in your midst and to help you bless others.

Friendship in Action

Plan your next birthday party around a service project and suggest presents that support the project.

More Than a Mentor

As iron sharpens iron, so a friend sharpens a friend.
PROVERBS 27:17

Erica paused at the door of the church, taking a deep breath before she stepped inside. She was excited about joining the youth group at her church, but she was also nervous. With kids ranging in age from middle to high school in the group—and having never spent much time with kids so much older than she was—she felt unsure about fitting in.

Despite her initial hesitance, she quickly felt welcomed. Within just a few weeks, she'd become friends with a girl named Chrissy. Her new friend was a junior, but despite the age gap, Chrissy went out of her way to spend time with Erica.

"Hey, do you want to go out to eat with us?" Chrissy asked her one night after youth group, motioning her over to a group of girls gathered off to the side. "You can ride with me. I'll drop you off afterward."

Erica's face lit up with excitement as she quickly checked with her stepdad about going with Chrissy.

After that, Chrissy often gave Erica rides to youth group events and included Erica in her circle of friends in a way that made her feel like a real friend, not a little kid tagging along.

Erica's friendship with Chrissy boosted her confidence and helped her sense she truly belonged in the group. It also helped set the tone for the rest of her time in youth group. Erica grew in her faith and began serving others. Years later, Erica continues to believe that Chrissy's friendship influenced both her relationship with God and the way she learned to treat friends of all ages.

The Bible reminds us that, as friends, we sharpen one another in the same way that iron does. When iron blades are rubbed together, they both become sharper. When our friends are good at spending time with God, being kind to others, and serving well, those good patterns and behaviors challenge us to act that way too. Just as iron makes iron more useful, good friends encourage us to be more effective.

Things to Think About

In what ways have your friends influenced or "sharpened" you in certain areas of your life?

Do you feel like you have helped influence your friends to grow in specific areas of their lives? Why or why not?

❀ DAILY ACT OF FRIENDSHIP ❀

Think of a friend or mentor who inspires you to be "sharpened" in a specific area of life. Make a list of a few friends you'd like to encourage in the same way.

Be You

JULIE

*You created my inmost being;
you knit me together in my mother's womb.*
PSALM 139:13, NIV

"I thought I'd hate Robotics, but it's really fun. Thanks for inviting me!" Allyson said as she, Christian, and Deshaun packed up their robotic station. "What shall we call our team?"

"Well, last year we were the Platypi, and we wore platypus costumes to all the meets. We took third place in state!" Christian grinned as he threw a gear at Deshaun.

"Hey, no throwing!" Deshaun said, catching the gear. "We decided that we need costumes again this year. They really helped us stand out from the other teams. You're okay with standing out, right?"

"Um, I think so! As long as we all wear the funny costumes together," Allyson replied.

"Oh, yeah. We'll all wear them and only to meets. Don't worry, it's a good time," Christian said.

As Allyson walked home, she prayed, *Jesus, thank you for sending friends who like me for being me. Help me never get caught in the popularity trap again. Amen.* Allyson skipped a step or two, grateful for how different her life was from only a year ago.

When Allyson started middle school, she wanted to be one of the popular kids. For a year, she tried hard to think, act, and look like the cool kids, but she was sad and miserable inside. Finally, instead of trying to change herself so she could fit in, Allyson looked for people who would accept her as she was. She found a group of friends who enjoyed the things she did, and she started to have fun when she didn't have to pretend anymore.

There is a lot of pressure to be things we are not, especially in middle and high school. You may feel pressure to pretend you aren't as smart as you actually are. You may be told your hobbies and interests are not cool. You may feel like you have to hide your faith. But Jesus knew what he was doing when he gave you your own talents and interests. He knew what he was doing when he made you shy or bold, quiet or loud, artistic or athletic. He has plans for you now and as an adult. Trust that Jesus knew exactly what he was doing when he made you.

Things to Think About

What makes you different from almost everyone else you know?

How might Jesus ask you to use your unique characteristics or talents to show the world his love?

❄ DAILY ACT OF FRIENDSHIP ❄

Make a list of your interests and hobbies.
Start a conversation with one person who likes
some of the same things you do.

Friendship in Action

Make a gratitude list of people or items you're thankful to have in your life.

About the Authors

After a 15-year career as a lawyer, Julie Fisk decided to follow her childhood dream of becoming an author. She shifted her storytelling from courtrooms and boardrooms to dinner tables and backyard barbecues, where she uncovers truth about faith, kindness, and friendship. Together with her cofounders of The Ruth Experience, Julie connects with thousands of women online through real, raw stories of living out faith. When she's not writing or speaking, you can find Julie with her husband and their two kids filling their home and backyard with friends.

Do it afraid. Kendra Roehl has sought to live out that advice as a social worker, foster parent, mother of five, and public speaker. She has a master's degree in social work and has naturally become a defender of those in need, serving others in hospice, low-income housing, and veterans' affairs programs. Kendra and her husband are well-known advocates for foster care, taking in more than twenty children in six years and adopting three of them. As a cofounder of The Ruth Experience, she continues to care for others as a frequent speaker and an author of five books.

A career in journalism set Kristin Demery up to one day publish her own stories of living this wild, precious life. She is now an author of five books and part of a trio of writers collectively known as The Ruth Experience. Kristin served as a newspaper and magazine editor, and her work has been featured in a variety of publications, including *USA Today*. She still works behind the scenes as an editor for others while writing her own series on kindness, friendship, and living with intention. An adventurer at heart, she loves checking items off the family bucket list with her husband and three daughters.

Join twelve-year-old Winnie Willis and her friends—both human and animal—on their adventures through paddock and pasture as they learn about caring for others, trusting God, and growing up.

Collect all eight Winnie the Horse Gentler books.
Or get the complete collection with the Barn Boxed Set!
(Eight books for the price of five.)

www.winniethehorsegentler.com

for GIRLS Only!
DEVOTIONS

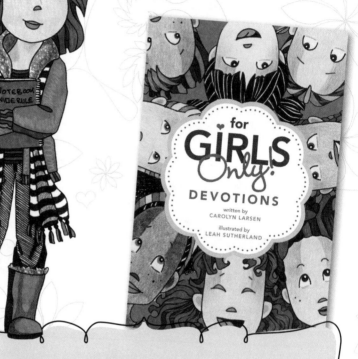

Feeling like you don't measure up? Dealing with gossip? Trying to face your fears? *For Girls Only!* gets right to the heart of all you're facing. Filled with Bible verses, stories about real issues, and self-quizzes, this devotional is a fun way to learn more about letting your light shine for Jesus every day.

For more information, visit www.tyndale.com/kids.

CP0386

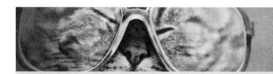

FOR ADVENTURERS

The Wormling series

Red Rock Mysteries series

FOR COMEDIANS

The Dead Sea Squirrels series

FOR ARTISTS

Made to Create with All My
Heart and Soul

Be Bold

FOR ANIMAL LOVERS

Winnie the Horse Gentler series

Starlight Animal Rescue series